ONE POT
COOKING

Published by Hinkler Books Pty Ltd
45–55 Fairchild Street
Heatherton Victoria 3202 Australia
www.hinkler.com.au

hinkler

Prepress: Splitting Image
Typesetting: MPS Ltd
Design: Pandemonium Creative
© A.C.N. 144 619 894 Pty Ltd 2011

ISBN: 978 1 7418 4100 8

Printed and bound in China

CONTENTS

INTRODUCTION

When you are planning a menu, whether it is for a dinner party, a casual barbecue or a weeknight family meal, you should always aim to make it as delicious and enjoyable as possible. It is important to contrast flavours, textures and ingredients.

There is something delicious about a meal that has stewed in a pot, the ingredients mixing lusciously together, releasing a flavour that is delectable and memorable.

One pot cooking is a simple way of delivering a hearty and flavourful meal. And while your ingredients are in the pot, you are free to prepare your accompaniments, other courses or desserts.

Pocket Chef One Pot Cooking provides you with delicious meals and side dishes that are appropriate for a casual or formal dinner occasion.

HOT BEEF BORSCHT

Preparation time:
30 minutes

Total cooking time:
2 hours 50 minutes

Serves 4–6

INGREDIENTS

- 500 g (1 lb 2 oz) gravy (boneless shin) beef, cut into large pieces
- 500 g (1 lb 2 oz) fresh beetroot (beet)
- 1 onion, finely chopped
- 1 carrot, cut into short strips
- 1 parsnip, cut into short strips
- 1 cup (75 g/2⅔ oz) finely shredded cabbage
- sour cream and chopped fresh chives, to serve

1. Put the beef and 1 litre (1.1 US qt/1.75 UK pt) water in a large, heavy-based saucepan, and bring slowly to the boil. Reduce the heat, cover and simmer for 1 hour. Skim the surface as required.

2. Cut the stems from the beetroot (beet), wash well and place in a large, heavy-based saucepan with 1 litre (1.1 US qt/1.75 UK pt) water. Bring to the boil, then reduce the heat and simmer for 40 minutes, or until tender. Drain, reserving 1 cup (250 ml/8½ fl oz) of the liquid. Cool, then peel and grate the beetroot (beet).

3. Remove the meat from the stock (broth), cool and dice. Skim any fat from the surface of the stock (broth). Return the meat to the stock (broth) and add the onion, carrot, parsnip, beetroot (beet) and reserved liquid. Bring to the boil, reduce the heat, cover and simmer for 45 minutes.

4. Stir in the cabbage and simmer for a further 15 minutes. Season to taste. Serve with the sour cream and chives.

LAMB HOTPOT

Preparation time:
40 minutes + 1 hour refrigeration

Total cooking time:
2 hours

Serves 4

INGREDIENTS

- 2 tablespoons olive oil
- 8 lamb shanks
- 2 onions, sliced
- 4 cloves garlic, finely chopped
- 3 bay leaves, torn in half
- 1–2 teaspoons hot paprika
- 2 teaspoons sweet paprika
- 1 tablespoon plain (all-purpose) flour
- ¼ cup (60 g/2 oz) tomato paste (tomato puree)
- 1.5 litres (1.6 US qt/1.3 UK qt) vegetable stock (broth)
- 4 potatoes, chopped
- 4 carrots, sliced
- 3 celery sticks (ribs), thickly sliced
- 3 tomatoes, seeded and chopped

1 To make the lamb stock (broth), heat 1 tablespoon of the oil in a large, heavy-based saucepan over medium heat. Brown the shanks well in two batches, then drain on paper towels.

2 Add the remaining oil to the pan and cook the onion, garlic and bay leaves over low heat for 10 minutes, stirring regularly. Add the paprikas and flour and cook, stirring, for 2 minutes. Gradually add the combined tomato paste (tomato puree) and vegetable stock (broth). Bring to the boil, stirring continuously, and return the shanks to the pan. Reduce the heat to low and simmer, covered, for 1½ hours, stirring occasionally.

3 Remove and discard the bay leaves. Remove the shanks, allow to cool slightly and then cut the meat from the bone. Discard the bone. Cut the meat into pieces and refrigerate. Refrigerate the stock (broth) for about 1 hour, or until fat forms on the surface and can be spooned off.

4 Return the meat to the stock (broth) along with the potato, carrot and celery, and bring to the boil. Reduce the heat and simmer for 15 minutes. Season, and add the chopped tomato to serve.

MULLIGATAWNY

Preparation time:
20 minutes

Total cooking time:
1 hour 15 minutes

Serves 4

INGREDIENTS

- 30 g (1 oz) butter
- 375 g (13¼ oz) chicken thigh cutlets, skin and fat removed
- 1 large onion, finely chopped
- 1 apple, peeled, cored and diced
- 1 tablespoon curry paste (jerk seasoning paste)

- 2 tablespoons plain (all-purpose) flour
- 3 cups (750 ml/26 fl oz) chicken stock (broth)
- ¼ cup (50 g/1¾ oz) basmati rice
- 1 tablespoon chutney
- 1 tablespoon lemon juice
- ¼ cup (60 ml/2 fl oz) cream

1 Heat the butter in a large heavy-based saucepan. Cook the chicken for 5 minutes, or until browned, then remove and set aside. Add the onion, apple and curry paste (jerk seasoning paste) to the pan. Cook for 5 minutes, or until the onion is soft. Stir in the flour and cook for 2 minutes, then add half the stock (broth). Stir until the mixture boils and thickens.

2 Return the chicken to the pan with the remaining stock (broth). Stir until boiling, then reduce the heat, cover and simmer for 1 hour. Add the rice for the last 15 minutes of cooking.

3 Remove the chicken from the pan. Remove the meat from the bones, dice finely and return to the pan. Add the chutney, lemon juice and cream, and season to taste.

LENTIL SOUP

Preparation time:	**Total cooking time:**	**Serves** 6
20 minutes + overnight refrigeration	3 hours 20 minutes	

INGREDIENTS

CHICKEN STOCK
- 1 kg (2 lb 3 oz) chicken bones (chicken necks, backs, wings), washed
- 1 small onion, roughly chopped
- 1 bay leaf
- 3–4 sprigs fresh flat-leaf parsley
- 1–2 sprigs fresh oregano or thyme
- 1½ cups (280 g/9¾ oz) brown lentils, washed

- 850 g (1 lb 14 oz) silverbeet (Swiss chard)
- ¼ cup (60 ml/2 fl oz) olive oil
- 1 large onion, finely chopped
- 4 cloves garlic, crushed
- ½ cup (25 g/¾ oz) finely chopped fresh coriander (cilantro) leaves
- ⅓ cup (80 ml/2¾ fl oz) lemon juice
- lemon wedges, to serve

1 To make the stock (broth), place all the ingredients in a large saucepan, add 3 litres (3.2 US qt/ 2.6 UK qt) water and bring to the boil. Skim any scum from the surface. Reduce the heat and simmer for 2 hours. Strain the stock (broth), discarding the bones, onion and herbs. Chill overnight. (You will need 1 litre/1.1 US qt/1.75 UK pt.)

2 Skim any fat from the stock (broth). Place the lentils in a large saucepan and add the stock (broth) and 1 litre (1.1 US qt/ 1.75 UK pt) water. Bring to the boil, then reduce the heat and simmer, covered, for 1 hour.

3 Meanwhile, remove the stems from the silverbeet (Swiss chard) and shred the leaves. Heat the oil in a saucepan over medium heat and cook the onion for 2–3 minutes, or until transparent. Add the garlic and cook for 1 minute. Add the silverbeet (Swiss chard) and toss for 2–3 minutes, or until wilted.

4 Stir the mixture into the lentils. Add the coriander (cilantro) and lemon juice, season and simmer, covered, for 15–20 minutes. Serve with the lemon wedges.

BARLEY SOUP WITH GOLDEN PARSNIPS

Preparation time:
30 minutes + overnight soaking

Total cooking time:
2 hours 20 minutes

Serves 6

INGREDIENTS

* 200 g (6½ oz) pearl barley
* 1 tablespoon oil
* 2 onions, chopped
* 2 cloves garlic, finely chopped
* 2 carrots, chopped
* 2 potatoes, chopped
* 2 celery sticks (ribs), chopped
* 2 bay leaves, torn in half
* 2 litres (2.1 US qt/1.75 UK qt) chicken stock (broth)
* ½ cup (125 ml/4¼ fl oz) milk
* 40 g (1½ oz) butter
* 3 parsnips, cubed
* 1 teaspoon soft brown sugar
* chopped fresh parsley, to serve

1 Soak the barley in water overnight. Drain. Place in a saucepan with 2 litres (2.1 US qt/1.75 UK qt) water. Bring to the boil, then reduce the heat and simmer, partially covered, for 1¼ hours, or until tender. Drain the barley.

2 Heat the oil in a large saucepan, add the onion, garlic, carrot, potato and celery, and cook for 3 minutes. Stir well and cook, covered, for 15 minutes over low heat, stirring occasionally.

3 Add the barley, bay leaves, stock (broth), milk, 2 teaspoons of salt and 1 teaspoon of pepper. Bring to the boil, then reduce the heat and simmer the soup, partially covered, for 35 minutes. If the soup is too thick, add about 1 cup (250 ml/8½ fl oz) cold water, a little at a time, until the soup reaches your preferred consistency.

4 While the soup is simmering, melt the butter in a frying pan, add the parsnip and toss in the butter. Sprinkle with the sugar and cook until golden brown and tender. Serve the parsnip on top of the soup and sprinkle with the parsley.

BEEF PHO

Preparation time:
15 minutes + 40 minutes freezing

Total cooking time:
30 minutes

Serves 4

INGREDIENTS

- 400 g (14 oz) rump steak, trimmed
- 1 litre (1.1 US qt/1.75 UK pt) beef stock (broth)
- ½ onion
- 1 star anise
- 1 cinnamon stick
- 1 tablespoon fish sauce
- pinch ground white pepper
- 200 g (7 oz) fresh thin round rice noodles
- 2 spring (green) onions, thinly sliced
- 30 fresh Vietnamese mint leaves
- 1 cup (90 g/3¼ oz) bean sprouts
- 1 small white onion, thinly sliced
- 1 small fresh red chilli, thinly sliced

1 Wrap the meat in plastic wrap and freeze for 30–40 minutes, or until partially frozen. Thinly slice the meat across the grain.

2 Place the stock (broth) in a large heavy-based saucepan with the onion half, star anise, cinnamon stick, fish sauce, white pepper and 2 cups (500 ml/17 fl oz) water, and bring to the boil over high heat. Reduce the heat to medium–low and simmer, covered, for 20 minutes. Discard the onion, star anise and cinnamon stick.

3 Meanwhile, cover the noodles with boiling water and gently separate. Drain and refresh with cold water. Divide the noodles and spring (green) onion among the serving bowls. Top with equal amounts of beef, mint, bean sprouts, onion slices and chilli. Ladle the simmering broth into the bowls, and serve.

NOTE: It is important that the broth is kept hot as the heat will cook the slices of beef.

MINESTRONE

Preparation time:
25 minutes + overnight
soaking

Total cooking time:
2 hours

Serves 6

INGREDIENTS

- 125 g (4⅓ oz) dried borlotti (romano) beans
- 1 large onion, roughly chopped
- 2 cloves garlic
- ¼ cup (7 g/¼ oz) roughly chopped fresh flat-leaf parsley
- 60 g (2 oz) pancetta, chopped
- ¼ cup (60 ml/2 fl oz) olive oil
- 1 celery stick (rib), halved lengthways, cut into 1 cm (½ inch) slices
- 1 carrot, halved lengthways, cut into 1 cm (½ inch) slices
- 1 potato, diced
- 2 teaspoons tomato paste (tomato puree)
- 400 g (14 oz) can diced tomatoes
- 6 fresh basil leaves, roughly torn
- 2 litres (2.1 US qt/1.75 UK qt) chicken or vegetable stock (broth)

- 2 thin zucchini (courgettes), cut into 1.5 cm (⅝ inch) slices
- ¾ cup (115 g/4 oz) shelled peas
- 60 g (2 oz) green beans, cut into 4 cm (1½ inch) lengths
- 80 g (2¾ oz) silverbeet (Swiss chard) leaves, shredded
- 75 g (2⅔ oz) ditalini or small pasta

PESTO
- 1 cup (30 g/1 oz) loosely packed fresh basil leaves
- 20 g (⅔ oz) lightly toasted pine nuts
- 2 cloves garlic
- 100 ml (3½ fl oz) olive oil
- ¼ cup (25 g/¾ oz) grated fresh Parmesan

1 Put the beans in a large bowl, cover with water and soak overnight. Drain and rinse under cold water.

2 Place the onion, garlic, parsley and pancetta in a food processor and process until finely chopped. Heat the oil in a saucepan, add the pancetta mixture and cook over low heat, stirring occasionally, for 8–10 minutes.

3 Add the celery, carrot and potato, and cook for 5 minutes, then stir in the tomato paste (tomato puree), tomato, basil and borlotti (romano) beans. Season with black pepper. Add the stock (broth) and bring slowly to the boil. Cover and simmer, stirring occasionally, for 1½ hours.

4 Season, and add the zucchini (courgettes), peas, green beans, silverbeet (Swiss chard) and pasta. Simmer for 8–10 minutes, or until the vegetables and pasta are al dente.

5 To make the pesto, combine the basil, pine nuts and garlic with a pinch of salt in a food processor. Process until finely chopped. With the motor running, slowly add the olive oil. Transfer to a bowl and stir in the Parmesan and ground black pepper to taste. Serve the soup in bowls with the pesto on top.

HOT AND SOUR SOUP

Preparation time:
40 minutes + overnight
refrigeration +
10 minutes standing

Total cooking time:
4 hours

Serves 6

INGREDIENTS

STOCK
- 1.5 kg (3 lb 5 oz) chicken bones
  (chicken necks, backs, wings), washed
- 2 slices fresh ginger (gingerroot),
  1 cm (½ inch) thick
- 4 spring (green) onions, white part only
- 200 g (7 oz) chicken breast fillet, cut
  into 2 cm (¾ inch) pieces
- 2 tablespoons garlic and red chilli paste
- ¼ cup (60 ml/2 fl oz) light soy sauce
- ¾ teaspoon ground white pepper
- 115 g (4 oz) baby corn, quartered
  lengthways
- ⅓ cup (80 ml/2¾ fl oz) Chinese
  black vinegar

- 4 fresh shiitake mushrooms, stems
  removed, caps thinly sliced
- 100 g (3½ oz) enoki mushrooms,
  trimmed and separated
- 65 g (2⅓ oz) fresh black wood fungus,
  cut into 1 cm (½ inch) strips
- 200 g (7 oz) fresh Shanghai noodles
- 200 g (7 oz) firm tofu, cut into
  2.5 cm (1 inch) cubes
- ¼ cup (30 g/1 oz) cornflour
  (cornstarch)
- 3 eggs, lightly beaten
- 1 teaspoon sesame oil
- 2 spring (green) onions, thinly sliced
  on the diagonal

1 To make the stock (broth),
place the bones and 3.5 litres
(3.7 US qt/3.1 UK qt) water in
a large saucepan and simmer – do
not boil. Cook for 30 minutes,
removing any scum as it rises to
the surface. Add the ginger

(gingerroot) and spring (green)
onion, and cook, partially
covered, at a low simmer for
3 hours. Strain through a fine sieve
and allow to cool. Cover and
refrigerate overnight. Remove
the layer of fat from the surface.

2 Bring 2 litres (2.1 US qt/
1.75 UK qt) of the stock (broth)
to the boil in a large saucepan
over high heat (freeze any
remaining stock). Reduce the
heat to medium, add the chicken,
garlic and chilli paste, soy sauce
and white pepper, and stir to
combine. Simmer, covered, for
10 minutes, or until the chicken
is cooked. Add the corn, vinegar,
mushrooms, wood fungus,
noodles and tofu. Season with
salt, and gently simmer for
5 minutes – do not stir.

3 Combine the cornflour
(cornstarch) and ¼ cup (60 ml/
2 fl oz) water. Slowly stir into the
soup until combined and slightly
thickened. Return to a simmer,
then pour the egg over the
surface in a very thin stream.
Turn off the heat, stand for
10 minutes, then stir in the
sesame oil. Garnish with the
spring (green) onion.

CANJA

Preparation time:
15 minutes

Total cooking time:
1 hour

Serves 6

INGREDIENTS

- 2.5 litres (2.6 US qt/2.2 UK qt) chicken stock (broth)
- 1 onion, cut into thin wedges
- 1 teaspoon grated lemon rind
- 1 sprig fresh mint
- 500 g (1 lb 2 oz) potatoes, chopped
- 1 tablespoon olive oil
- 2 chicken breast fillets
- 1 cup (200 g/7 oz) long-grain rice
- 2 tablespoons lemon juice
- fresh shredded mint, to garnish

1 Combine the chicken stock (broth), onion, lemon rind, mint sprig, potato and olive oil in a large saucepan. Slowly bring to the boil, then reduce the heat, add the chicken breasts and simmer gently for 20–25 minutes, or until the chicken is cooked through.

2 Remove the chicken breasts and discard the mint sprig. Cool the chicken, then cut it into thin slices.

3 Meanwhile, add the rice to the pan and simmer for 25–30 minutes, or until the rice is tender. Return the sliced chicken to the pan, add the lemon juice and stir for 1–2 minutes, or until the chicken is warmed through. Season, and serve garnished with mint.

NOTE: Rice and potato absorb liquid on standing, so serve immediately.

CLAM CHOWDER

Preparation time:
25 minutes

Total cooking time:
45 minutes

Serves 4

INGREDIENTS

- 30 g (1 oz) butter
- 2 rashers bacon, finely chopped
- 1 large onion, finely chopped
- 4 potatoes, cut into small cubes
- 2 cups (500 ml/17 fl oz) fish stock (broth)
- 1 bay leaf

- ½ cup (125 ml/4¼ fl oz) milk
- 4 x 105 g (3⅔ oz) cans baby clams, drained and chopped (see NOTE)
- ¼ cup (15 g/½ oz) finely chopped fresh parsley
- 1 cup (250 ml/8½ fl oz) cream

1 Heat the butter in a large saucepan. Cook the bacon and onion for 2–3 minutes, or until softened. Stir in the potato. Cook for a further 2–3 minutes, then gradually pour on the stock (broth). Add the bay leaf.

2 Bring the mixture to the boil, then reduce the heat and simmer, covered, for 20 minutes, or until the potato is cooked. Simmer for 10 minutes, or until the soup is reduced and slightly thickened. Discard the bay leaf.

3 Add the milk, chopped clams, parsley and cream. Stir to reheat, but do not allow the soup to boil. Season with salt and freshly ground black pepper.

NOTE: Baby clams can be replaced with seafood mix to make a seafood chowder.

SPICED BEEF AND POTATOES

Preparation time:
15 minutes

Total cooking time:
1 hour 40 minutes

Serves 4

INGREDIENTS

SPICE PASTE
• 2 onions, chopped
• 2 cloves garlic, chopped
• 2 teaspoons grated lemon rind
• 2 small fresh red chillies, chopped
• 2 teaspoons ground coriander
• 2 teaspoons ground cumin
• 1 teaspoon ground turmeric
• ½ teaspoon ground cardamom
• 1 teaspoon garam masala

• 2 tablespoons oil
• 1 kg (2 lb 3 oz) lean chuck steak, cut into 3 cm (1¼ inch) cubes
• ¾ cup (185 ml/6½ fl oz) coconut cream
• 1 tablespoon tamarind sauce
• 500 g (1 lb 2 oz) baby potatoes, halved

1 To make the spice paste, combine all the ingredients in a food processor or blender, and process for 1 minute, or until very finely chopped.

2 Heat the oil in a heavy-based saucepan. Cook the meat quickly in small batches over medium–high heat until well browned. Drain on paper towels.

3 Add the spice paste to the pan and stir over medium heat for 2 minutes. Return the meat to the pan with the coconut cream, tamarind sauce and ½ cup (125 ml/4¼ fl oz) water, and bring to the boil. Reduce the heat to a simmer and cook, covered, for 30 minutes, stirring occasionally.

4 Add the potato and cook, covered, for 30 minutes. Remove the lid and cook for 30 minutes, or until the meat is tender and almost all of the liquid has evaporated.

NAVARIN OF LAMB

Preparation time:
25 minutes

Total cooking time:
1 hour 35 minutes

Serves 4

INGREDIENTS

- 8 lamb noisettes (see NOTES)
- seasoned plain (all-purpose) flour
- 2 tablespoons oil
- 2 celery sticks (ribs), sliced
  diagonally into 2 cm (¾ inch) lengths
- 12 baby carrots, peeled
  (see NOTES)
- 12 new potatoes
- 6 sprigs fresh thyme
- ¼ cup (15 g/½ oz) chopped
  fresh parsley
- 2 onions, chopped
- 2 cloves garlic, crushed
- ⅓ cup (40 g/1¼ oz) plain
  (all-purpose) flour
- 2½ cups (625 ml/21 fl oz) chicken
  stock (broth)
- 1 cup (250 ml/8½ fl oz) red wine
- ¼ cup (60 g/2 oz) tomato paste
  (tomato puree)
- chopped fresh parsley, extra,
  to garnish

1 Toss the lamb in the seasoned
   flour, shaking off the excess.
   Preheat the oven to moderate
   180°C (350°F/Gas 4).

2 Heat the oil in a heavy-based
   saucepan. In batches, brown the
   lamb well on both sides over
   medium–high heat. Remove
   from the heat, drain well on
   paper towels, then transfer to
   a greased, 3 litre (3.2 US qt/
   2.6 UK qt) casserole dish. Top
   with the celery, carrots, potatoes,
   thyme and parsley.

3 Cook the onion and garlic in
   the same heavy-based pan,
   stirring over medium heat for
   5–10 minutes, or until the
   onion is soft.

4 Add the flour and stir for
   1 minute, or until the onion is
   coated. Add the remaining
   ingredients and stir until the
   sauce boils and thickens. Pour
   the sauce over the lamb and
   vegetables. Bake, covered, for
   1¼ hours, or until the lamb is
   tender. Carefully remove the
   string from the lamb, and sprinkle
   with extra parsley to serve.

NOTES: A noisette is a round slice of meat, cut from a boned loin and tied with string to hold its shape. For this recipe you could also use a boned leg of lamb, cut into 3 cm (1¼ inch) cubes.

If baby carrots are not available, use four sliced carrots instead.

PORK STEW

Preparation time:
15 minutes + overnight marinating

Total cooking time:
1 hour 20 minutes

Serves 4–6

INGREDIENTS

- 1½ tablespoons coriander seeds
- 800 g (1 lb 12 oz) pork fillet, cut into 2 cm (¾ inch) cubes
- 1 tablespoon plain (all-purpose) flour
- ¼ cup (60 ml/2 fl oz) olive oil
- 1 large onion, thinly sliced
- 1½ cups (375 ml/13 fl oz) red wine
- 1 cup (250 ml/8½ fl oz) chicken stock (broth)
- 1 teaspoon sugar
- sprigs fresh coriander (cilantro), to garnish

1 Crush the coriander seeds in a mortar and pestle. Combine the pork, crushed seeds and ½ teaspoon cracked black pepper in a bowl. Cover and marinate overnight in the refrigerator.

2 Combine the flour and pork, and toss to coat. Heat 2 tablespoons of the oil in a saucepan and cook the pork in batches over high heat for 1–2 minutes, or until brown. Remove.

3 Heat the remaining oil, add the onion and cook over medium heat for 2–3 minutes, or until just golden. Return the meat to the pan, add the red wine, stock (broth) and sugar, and season. Bring to the boil, then reduce the heat and simmer, covered, for 1 hour.

4 Remove the meat. Return the pan to the heat and boil over high heat for 3–5 minutes, or until the liquid is reduced and slightly thickened. Pour over the meat and top with coriander (cilantro).

BEEF BOURGUIGNONNE

Preparation time:
10 minutes

Total cooking time:
2 hours

Serves 4

INGREDIENTS

- 1 kg (2 lb 3 oz) diced beef
- ¼ cup (30 g/1 oz) seasoned plain (all-purpose) flour
- 1 tablespoon oil
- 150 g (5¼ oz) bacon, diced
- 8 bulb spring (green) onions, greens trimmed to 2 cm (¾ inch)
- 200 g (7 oz) button mushrooms
- 2 cups (500 ml/17 fl oz) red wine
- 2 tablespoons tomato paste (tomato puree)
- 2 cups (500 ml/17 fl oz) beef stock (broth)
- 1 bouquet garni (see NOTE)

1 Toss the beef in the seasoned flour until evenly coated, shaking off any excess. Heat the oil in a large saucepan over high heat. Cook the beef in three batches for about 3 minutes, or until well browned all over, adding a little extra oil as needed. Remove from the pan.

2 Add the bacon to the pan and cook for 2 minutes, or until browned. Remove with a slotted spoon and add to the beef. Add the spring (green) onions and mushrooms, and cook for 5 minutes, or until the onions are browned. Remove.

3 Slowly pour the red wine into the pan, scraping up any sediment from the bottom with a wooden spoon. Stir in the tomato paste (tomato puree) and stock (broth). Add the bouquet garni and return the beef, bacon and any juices. Bring to the boil, then reduce the heat and simmer for 45 minutes. Return the spring (green) onions and mushrooms to the pan. Cook for 1 hour, or until the meat is very tender and the sauce is glossy. Serve with steamed new potatoes or mash.

NOTE: To make a bouquet garni, wrap the green part of a leek around a bay leaf, a sprig of thyme, a sprig of parsley and celery leaves, and tie with string. The combination of herbs can be varied according to taste.

MADRID CHICKEN

Preparation time:
10 minutes

Total cooking time:
1 hour

Serves 4

INGREDIENTS

- 1 orange
- 1 tablespoon olive oil
- 4 chicken breasts (skin and excess fat removed)
- 2 chorizo sausages (about 200 g/ 7 oz), cut into 1 cm (½ inch) slices
- 1 cup (250 ml/8½ fl oz) chicken stock (broth)
- 1 cup (250 g/8¾ oz) bottled tomato pasta (marinara) sauce
- 12 Kalamata olives
- Kalamata olives, extra, to garnish
- fresh flat-leaf parsley, to garnish

1 Using a vegetable peeler, carefully cut 4 thin strips of orange rind (about 1 × 4 cm/½ × 1½ inches). Remove the peel and pith from the orange, and segment the flesh.

2 Heat the oil in a saucepan and brown the chicken and chorizo slices, in batches if necessary. (Leave the meat side of the chicken browning for 5 minutes.) Add the stock (broth), tomato (marinara) sauce and orange rind. Bring to the boil, then reduce the heat and simmer, covered, for 25 minutes.

3 Remove the lid, turn the chicken over and continue to simmer, uncovered, for about 25 minutes, or until the chicken is tender and the sauce reduced. Season with salt and freshly ground black pepper, and stir through the olives and orange segments. Garnish with extra olives and flat-leaf parsley.

NOTE: Chorizo sausages can be replaced with any spicy sausages.

LAMB HOTPOT
WITH NOODLES

Preparation time:
20 minutes + 2 hours
marinating

Total cooking time:
2 hours

Serves 4

INGREDIENTS

- 2 cloves garlic, crushed
- 2 teaspoons grated fresh ginger (gingerroot)
- 1 teaspoon five-spice powder
- ¼ teaspoon ground white pepper
- 2 tablespoons Chinese rice wine
- 1 teaspoon sugar
- 1 kg (2 lb 3 oz) boneless lamb shoulder, trimmed and cut into 3 cm (1¼ inch) pieces
- 30 g (1 oz) whole dried Chinese mushrooms
- 1 tablespoon peanut oil
- 1 large onion, cut into wedges
- 2 cm (¾ inch) piece fresh ginger (gingerroot), julienned
- 1 teaspoon Sichuan peppercorns, crushed or ground

- 2 tablespoons sweet bean paste
- 1 teaspoon black peppercorns, ground and toasted
- 2 cups (500 ml/17 fl oz) chicken stock (broth)
- ¼ cup (60 ml/2 fl oz) oyster sauce
- 2 star anise
- ¼ cup (60 ml/2 fl oz) Chinese rice wine, extra
- 80 g (2¾ oz) can sliced bamboo shoots
- 100 g (3½ oz) can water chestnuts, drained and sliced
- 400 g (14 oz) fresh rice noodles, cut into 2 cm (¾ inch) wide strips
- 1 spring (green) onion, sliced on the diagonal

1 Combine the garlic, grated ginger (gingerroot), five-spice powder, white pepper, rice wine, sugar and 1 teaspoon salt in a large bowl. Add the lamb and toss to coat. Cover and marinate for 2 hours.

2 Meanwhile, soak the mushrooms in boiling water for 20 minutes. Drain. Discard the stems and slice the caps.

3 Heat a wok over high heat, add the oil and swirl to coat. Stir-fry (scramble-fry) the onion, julienned ginger (gingerroot) and Sichuan pepper for 2 minutes. Cook the lamb in three batches, stir-frying (scramble-frying) for 2–3 minutes each batch, or until starting to brown. Return all the lamb to the wok. Stir in the bean paste and black peppercorns, and cook for 3 minutes, or until the lamb is brown.

4 Add the stock (broth) and transfer to a 2 litre (2.1 US qt/ 1.75 UK qt) flameproof clay pot or casserole dish. Stir in the oyster sauce, star anise and extra rice wine and simmer, covered, over low heat for 1½ hours, or until the lamb is tender. Stir in the drained bamboo shoots and water chestnuts, and cook for 20 minutes. Add the mushrooms.

5 Cover the noodles with boiling water and gently separate. Drain and rinse the noodles, then add to the hotpot, stirring for 1–2 minutes, or until heated through. Serve sprinkled with spring (green) onion.

STEAK AND KIDNEY STEW

Preparation time:
35 minutes

Total cooking time:
2 hours 30 minutes

Serves 4–6

INGREDIENTS

- 1 kg (2 lb 3 oz) chuck steak, trimmed
- 8 lamb's kidneys
- ¼ cup (60 ml/2 fl oz) oil
- 1 rasher bacon, rind removed, cut into long, thin strips
- 40 g (1½ oz) butter
- 1 large onion, chopped
- 300 g (10½ oz) button mushrooms, halved
- 1 cup (250 ml/8½ fl oz) Muscat
- 2–3 cloves garlic, crushed
- ¼ teaspoon ground allspice
- ½ teaspoon paprika
- 2 teaspoons coriander seeds, lightly crushed
- 1 tablespoon wholegrain mustard
- 1 cup (250 ml/8½ fl oz) beef stock (broth)
- 2–3 tablespoons soft brown sugar
- 1–2 teaspoons fresh thyme
- 1–2 teaspoons fresh rosemary

1 Cut the steak into 2.5 cm (1 inch) cubes. Cut the kidneys in half, remove the core and any fat, then slice them in half again.

2 Heat 1 teaspoon of the oil in a large, heavy-based saucepan. Add the bacon and cook over medium heat until just crisp. Remove and set aside.

3 Heat 2 tablespoons of the oil and 30 g (1 oz) of the butter in the pan. Brown the steak cubes in batches, then set aside.

4 Add the onion to the pan and cook for 3 minutes, or until soft and golden. Add the mushrooms and cook, stirring, for 3 minutes, until starting to brown. Stir in half the Muscat and simmer for 3–4 minutes. Remove and set aside.

5 Add the remaining oil and butter to the pan. Stir in the garlic, allspice, paprika and coriander, and cook for 1 minute. Add the kidney and cook until just starting to brown. Stir in the mustard and remaining Muscat, and simmer for 2 minutes.

6 Stir in the bacon, steak, onion and mushrooms. Stir in the stock (broth), bring to the boil, then reduce the heat, cover and simmer for 1 hour. Add the sugar. Simmer, covered, for 40 minutes, then uncovered for 20 minutes, stirring in the herbs during the last 10 minutes.

LAMB KEFTA

Preparation time:
30 minutes

Total cooking time:
40 minutes

Serves 4

INGREDIENTS

- 1 kg (2 lb 3 oz) lamb mince (ground lamb)
- 1 onion, finely chopped
- 2 cloves garlic, finely chopped
- 2 tablespoons finely chopped fresh flat-leaf parsley
- 2 tablespoons finely chopped fresh coriander (cilantro) leaves
- ½ teaspoon cayenne (red) pepper
- ½ teaspoon ground allspice
- ½ teaspoon ground ginger
- ½ teaspoon ground cardamom
- 1 teaspoon ground cumin
- 1 teaspoon paprika

SAUCE
- 2 tablespoons olive oil
- 1 onion, finely chopped
- 2 cloves garlic, finely chopped
- 2 teaspoons ground cumin
- ½ teaspoon ground cinnamon
- 1 teaspoon paprika
- 2 × 425 g (15 oz) cans chopped tomatoes
- 2 teaspoons harissa (hot chilli [pepper] sauce)
- ⅓ cup (20 g/⅔ oz) chopped fresh coriander (cilantro) leaves

1 Preheat the oven to moderate 180°C (350°F/Gas 4). Lightly grease two baking trays (sheets). Place the lamb, onion, garlic, herbs and spices in a bowl, and mix together well. Season with salt and pepper. Roll tablespoons of the mixture into balls and place on the trays (sheets). Bake for 18–20 minutes, or until browned.

2 Meanwhile, to make the sauce, heat the oil in a large saucepan, add the onion and cook over medium heat for 5 minutes, or until soft. Add the garlic, cumin, cinnamon and paprika, and cook for 1 minute, or until fragrant.

3 Stir in the tomato and harissa, and bring to the boil. Reduce the heat and simmer for 20 minutes, then add the meatballs and simmer for 10 minutes, or until cooked through. Stir in the coriander (cilantro), season well, and serve.

PORK HOTPOT

Preparation time:
20 minutes

Total cooking time:
1 hour 40 minutes

Serves 4

INGREDIENTS

- olive oil, for cooking
- 375 g (13¼ oz) slender eggplant (aubergine), cut into 3 cm (1¼ inch) slices
- 8 bulb spring (green) onions
- 400 g (14 oz) can chopped tomatoes
- 2 cloves garlic, crushed
- 2 teaspoons ground cumin
- 500 g (1 lb 2 oz) pork fillet, cut into 3 cm (1¼ inch) thick slices
- seasoned plain (all-purpose) flour
- ⅔ cup (170 ml/5¾ fl oz) cider
- 1 sprig fresh rosemary
- 2 tablespoons finely chopped toasted almonds

1 Heat ¼ cup (60 ml/2 fl oz) of oil in a large, heavy-based frying pan. Brown the eggplant (aubergine) in batches in high heat, adding oil as needed. Remove and set aside.

2 Quarter the spring (green) onions along their length. Add some oil to the pan and fry the spring (green) onion over medium heat for 5 minutes. Add the tomato, garlic and cumin, and cook for 2 minutes. Remove and set aside.

3 Coat the pork in the seasoned flour, shaking off any excess. Brown in batches over medium–high heat until golden, adding oil as needed. Remove and set aside.

4 Add the cider to the pan and stir well, scraping down the side and base. Allow to boil for 1–2 minutes, then add ½ cup (125 ml/4¼ fl oz) water. Reduce the heat and stir in the spring (green) onion and tomato. Add the pork, season, and poke the rosemary sprig into the stew. Partially cover and simmer gently for 20 minutes.

5 Layer the eggplant (aubergine) on top, partially cover and cook for 25 minutes, or until the pork is tender. Just before serving, gently toss the almonds through.

LAMB'S LIVER STEW

Preparation time:
10 minutes

Total cooking time:
30 minutes

Serves 6

INGREDIENTS

- 1 lamb's liver, about 750 g
  (1 lb 10 oz) (see NOTE)
- ¼ cup (30 g/1 oz)
  cornflour (cornstarch)
- ¼ teaspoon ground black pepper
- 6 rashers bacon, cut into
  large pieces
- 2 tablespoons oil
- 2 onions, thinly sliced
- 1 beef stock (bouillon)
  cube, crumbled

1 Wash the liver and cut it into thin slices, discarding any veins or discoloured spots. Pat the liver dry with paper towels. Combine the cornflour (cornstarch) and pepper. Toss the liver slices in the seasoned cornflour (cornstarch), shaking off the excess.

2 Cook the bacon in a heavy-based saucepan until crisp, then drain on paper towels. Heat the oil in the pan and cook the onion gently until golden, then remove from the pan.

3 Cook the liver quickly in small batches over medium heat until well browned, then drain on paper towels. Return the liver, bacon and onion to the pan. Dissolve the stock (bouillon) cube in 1 cup (250 ml/ 8½ fl oz) boiling water, then gradually add to the pan. Stir over medium heat for 10 minutes, or until the liquid boils and thickens. Serve the stew immediately.

NOTE: Soaking the liver in milk for 30 minutes before cooking will result in a milder taste.

GARLIC SEAFOOD STEW

Preparation time:
20 minutes

Total cooking time:
20 minutes

Serves 6

INGREDIENTS

- 12 scallops, with roe
- 500 g (1 lb 2 oz) skinless firm white fish fillets (see NOTE)
- 6 raw slipper lobsters or crabs
- 500 g (1 lb 2 oz) raw medium prawns (shrimp)
- 50 g (1¾ oz) butter
- 1 onion, finely chopped

- 5–6 large cloves garlic, finely chopped
- ½ cup (125 ml/4¼ fl oz) white wine
- 2 cups (500 ml/17 fl oz) cream
- 1½ tablespoons Dijon mustard
- 2 teaspoons lemon juice
- 2 tablespoons chopped fresh flat-leaf parsley

1 Slice or pull off any membrane or hard muscle from the scallops. Cut the fish into 2 cm (¾ inch) cubes. Cut the heads off the slipper lobsters or crabs, then use kitchen scissors to cut down around the sides of the tail so you can flap open the shell. Remove the flesh in one piece, then slice each piece in half. Peel and devein the prawns (shrimps). Refrigerate all the seafood, covered, until ready to use.

2 Melt the butter in a frying pan and cook the onion and garlic over medium heat for 2 minutes, or until the onion is softened (be careful not to burn the garlic – it may turn bitter).

3 Add the wine to the pan and cook for 4 minutes, or until reduced by half. Stir in the cream, mustard and lemon juice, and simmer for 5–6 minutes, or until reduced to almost half.

4 Add the prawns (shrimp) to the pan and cook for 1 minute, then add the slipper lobster or crab meat and cook for another minute, or until white. Add the fish and cook for 2 minutes, or until cooked through (the flesh will flake easily when tested with a fork). Finally, add the scallops and cook for 1 minute. If any of the seafood is still not cooked, cook for another minute or so, but be careful not to overcook as this will result in tough flesh. Remove the frying pan from the heat and toss the parsley through. Season to taste. Serve with salad and bread.

NOTE: Try using perch, ling, bream, tuna or blue-eye.

GREEK OCTOPUS STEW

Preparation time:
25 minutes

Total cooking time:
1 hour 10 minutes

Serves 4–6

INGREDIENTS

- 1 kg (2 lb 3 oz) baby octopus
- 2 tablespoons olive oil
- 1 large onion, chopped
- 3 cloves garlic, crushed
- 1 bay leaf
- 3 cups (750 ml/26 fl oz) red wine
- ¼ cup (60 ml/2 fl oz) red wine vinegar
- 400 g (14 oz) can crushed tomatoes
- 1 tablespoon tomato paste (tomato puree)
- 1 tablespoon chopped fresh oregano
- ¼ teaspoon ground cinnamon
- small pinch ground cloves
- 1 teaspoon sugar
- 2 tablespoons finely chopped fresh flat-leaf parsley

1 Cut between the head and tentacles of the octopus, just below the eyes. Grasp the body and push the beak out and up through the centre of the tentacles with your fingers. Cut the eyes from the head by slicing off a small round. Discard the eye section. Carefully slit through one side, avoiding the ink sac, and remove any gut from inside. Rinse the octopus well under running water.

2 Heat the oil in a large saucepan, add the onion and cook over medium heat for 5 minutes, or until starting to brown. Add the garlic and bay leaf, and cook for 1 minute further. Add the octopus and stir to coat in the onion mixture.

3 Stir in the wine, vinegar, tomato, tomato paste (tomato puree), oregano, cinnamon, cloves and sugar. Bring to the boil, then reduce the heat and simmer for 1 hour, or until the octopus is tender and the sauce has thickened slightly. Stir in the parsley and season with salt and ground black pepper. Serve with a Greek salad and crusty bread to mop up the delicious juices.

MEXICAN BEEF STEW

Preparation time:
30 minutes

Total cooking time:
1 hour 30 minutes

Serves 6

INGREDIENTS

- 500 g (1 lb 2 oz) Roma
  tomatoes, halved
- 6 flour tortillas
- 1–2 fresh red chillies,
  finely chopped
- 1 tablespoon olive oil
- 1 kg (2 lb 3 oz) stewing beef, cubed
- ½ teaspoon black pepper
- 2 onions, thinly sliced
- 1½ cups (375 ml/13 fl oz) beef
  stock (broth)
- ¼ cup (60 g/2 oz) tomato paste
  (tomato puree)
- 375 g (13¼ oz) can red kidney
  beans, drained
- 1 teaspoon chilli powder
- ½ cup (125 g/4⅓ oz) sour cream

1 Preheat the oven to moderate
   180°C (350°F/Gas 4). Grill
   the tomatoes, skin-side up,
   under a hot grill (broiler) for

6–8 minutes, or until the skin is
black and blistered. Cool,
remove the skin and roughly
chop the flesh.

2 Bake 2 of the tortillas for 4
   minutes, or until crisp. Break into
   pieces and put in a food
   processor with the tomato and
   chilli. Process for 30 seconds, or
   until almost smooth.

3 Heat the oil in a large heavy-based
   saucepan. Brown the beef in
   batches, season with pepper, then
   remove. Add the onion to the pan
   and cook for 5 minutes. Return
   the meat to the pan. Stir in the
   processed mixture, stock (broth)
   and tomato paste (tomato puree),
   and bring to the boil. Reduce
   the heat, cover and simmer for
   1¼ hours. Add the beans and chilli
   powder, and heat through.

4 Grill (broil) the remaining
   tortillas for 2–3 minutes on each
   side, then cool and cut into
   wedges. Serve the stew with the
   sour cream, and toasted tortilla
   wedges on the side.

HINT: If this stew becomes thick
during cooking, thin it with a little
extra stock.

BRAISED PORK STEW

Preparation time:
15 minutes
Total cooking time:
30 minutes
Serves 4

INGREDIENTS

- 4 lean pork loin medallions, about 175 g (6¼ oz) each
- 2 cups (500 ml/17 fl oz) chicken stock (broth)
- 2 tablespoons oil
- 1 large onion, cut into wedges
- 2 cloves garlic, crushed
- 1 tablespoon fresh thyme leaves
- 1 large tomato, peeled, seeded and finely chopped
- ½ cup (125 ml/4¼ fl oz) cream
- 16 pitted prunes (dried plums)

1 Shape the meat into rounds by securing a length of string around the medallions. Tie with a bow for easy removal. Bring the stock (broth) to the boil in a medium saucepan. Reduce the heat to a simmer and cook for 5 minutes, or until reduced to ¾ cup (185 ml/6½ fl oz).

2 Heat the oil over high heat in a heavy-based frying pan. Cook the meat for 2 minutes each side to seal, turning once. Drain on paper towels.

3 Add the onion and garlic to the saucepan, and stir for 2 minutes. Return the meat to the pan with the thyme, tomato and stock (broth), then reduce the heat to low. Cover the pan and bring slowly to simmering point. Simmer for 10 minutes, or until the meat is tender, turning once. Add the cream and prunes (dried plums), and simmer for a further 5 minutes.

MOROCCAN SEAFOOD STEW

Preparation time:	**Total cooking time:**	**Serves** 6
50 minutes	50 minutes	

INGREDIENTS

- 2 tablespoons olive oil
- 2 red onions, roughly chopped
- 1 red capsicum (pepper), chopped
- 4 cloves garlic, crushed
- 2 teaspoons ground cumin
- 1 teaspoon ground coriander
- 2 teaspoons sweet paprika
- ½ teaspoon dried chilli flakes
- 1 cup (250 ml/8½ fl oz) chicken or fish stock (broth)
- 425 g (15 oz) can chopped tomatoes
- ⅓ cup (80 ml/2¾ fl oz) orange juice
- 1 tablespoon sugar
- ¼ cup (40 g/1½ oz) seedless raisins (dark raisins)

- 375 g (13¼ oz) baby new potatoes
- 500 g (1 lb 2 oz) baby octopus, cleaned
- 12 raw king prawns (shrimp), peeled and deveined, tails intact
- 1 kg (2 lb 3 oz) thick white fish fillets, cut into chunks

PUREE
- 1 cup (30 g/1 oz) fresh coriander (cilantro) leaves
- 2 tablespoons ground almonds
- ⅓ cup (80 ml/2¾ fl oz) extra virgin olive oil
- ½ teaspoon ground cumin
- 1 teaspoon honey

1 Heat the olive oil in a large saucepan and cook the onion over medium heat for about 5 minutes, or until soft. Add the capsicum (pepper) and garlic, and cook for another minute. Add the cumin, coriander, paprika and chilli flakes, and cook until fragrant.

2 Pour in the stock (broth), tomato, orange juice, sugar and raisins (dark raisins), and bring to the boil. Add the potatoes, reduce the heat to low and gently simmer for 20–30 minutes, or until the potatoes are just tender. Season to taste.

3 Use a small sharp knife to remove the octopus heads; slit the heads open and remove the gut. Grasp the body firmly and push the beak out with your index finger; remove and discard. Add the octopus, prawns (shrimps) and fish to the pan and cook, covered, for 10 minutes, or until the fish flakes when tested with a fork.

4 To make the puree, place the coriander (cilantro) leaves and ground almonds in a food processor. With the motor running, drizzle in the oil and process until smooth, then add the cumin, honey and salt to taste. Process until well combined.

5 To serve, dish the stew onto serving plates and drizzle a spoonful of puree on top. Serve with couscous and a green leaf salad.

SPANISH CHICKEN STEW

Preparation time:
10 minutes

Total cooking time:
1 hour

Serves 4

INGREDIENTS

- ¼ cup (60 ml/2 fl oz) olive oil
- 4 chicken thighs and 6 drumsticks
- 1 large red onion, finely chopped
- 1 large green capsicum
  (pepper), two-thirds diced and
  one-third julienned
- 3 teaspoons sweet paprika
- 400 g (14 oz) can diced tomatoes
- 1¼ cups (275 g/9⅔ oz) paella or
  arborio rice (see NOTE)
- ½ teaspoon ground saffron

1 Heat 2 tablespoons of the oil in a
  large deep frying pan over high
  heat. Season the chicken pieces
  well and brown in batches.
  Remove the chicken from
  the pan.

2 Reduce the heat to medium and
  add the remaining oil. Add the
  onion and the diced capsicum
  (pepper), and cook gently for
  5 minutes. Stir in the sweet
  paprika and cook for 30 seconds.
  Add the tomato and simmer for
  1–3 minutes, or until it thickens.

3 Stir in 3½ cups (875 ml/30 fl oz)
  boiling water, then add the rice
  and saffron. Return the chicken
  to the pan and stir to combine.
  Season to taste. Bring to the boil,
  then cover, reduce the heat to
  medium–low and simmer for
  20–30 minutes, or until the
  liquid has been absorbed and
  the chicken is tender. Stir in the
  julienned capsicum (pepper),
  then allow to stand, covered, for
  3–4 minutes before serving.

NOTE: Paella rice is a medium
round grain from Spain. Calasparra
is the most commonly available
variety and can be purchased from
fine food stores or delicatessens.

STUFFED SQUID STEW

Preparation time:
50 minutes

Total cooking time:
50 minutes

Serves 4

INGREDIENTS

- 100 ml (3½ fl oz) olive oil
- 1 large onion, finely chopped
- 2 cloves garlic, crushed
- 1 cup (80 g/2¾ oz) fresh breadcrumbs
- 1 egg, lightly beaten
- 60 g (2 oz) kefalotyri cheese, grated
- 60 g (2 oz) haloumi cheese, grated
- 4 large or 8 small squid (1 kg/2 lb 3 oz), cleaned (see NOTE)
- 1 small onion, finely chopped, extra
- 2 cloves garlic, crushed, extra
- 500 g (1 lb 2 oz) firm ripe tomatoes, peeled and diced
- 150 ml (5 fl oz) red wine
- 1 tablespoon chopped fresh oregano
- 1 tablespoon chopped fresh flat-leaf parsley

1 Heat 2 tablespoons of the oil in a frying pan, add the onion and cook over medium heat for 3 minutes. Remove. Combine with the garlic, breadcrumbs, egg and cheese. Season.

2 Pat the squid hoods dry with paper towels and, using a teaspoon, fill them three-quarters full with the stuffing. Do not pack them too tightly or the stuffing mixture will swell and burst out during cooking. Secure the ends with wooden toothpicks.

3 Heat the remaining oil in a large frying pan, add the squid and cook for 1–2 minutes on all sides. Remove. Add the extra onion and cook over medium heat for 3 minutes, or until soft, then add the extra garlic and cook for a further 1 minute. Stir in the tomato and wine, and simmer for 10 minutes, or until thick and pulpy, then stir in the oregano and parsley. Return the squid to the pan and cook, covered, for 20–25 minutes, or until tender. Serve warm with the tomato sauce or cool with a salad.

NOTE: Ask the fishmonger to clean the squid. Or, discard the tentacles and cartilage. Rinse the hoods under running water and pull off the skin.

CREAMY PORK STEW

Preparation time:
20 minutes

Total cooking time:
2 hours

Serves 4

INGREDIENTS

- 750 g (1 lb 10 oz) pork steaks, cut into 1 cm (½ inch) strips
- ¼ cup (30 g/1 oz) plain (all-purpose) flour
- 30 g (1 oz) butter
- 1 clove garlic, crushed
- 1 tablespoon Dijon mustard
- 1 cup (250 ml/8½ fl oz) cream
- ½ cup (125 ml/4¼ fl oz) white wine
- 1 tablespoon chopped fresh thyme
- 1 cup (250 ml/8½ fl oz) chicken stock (broth)
- 375 g (13¼ oz) button mushrooms, halved

1 Toss the meat in the flour, shaking off the excess. Heat the butter and garlic in a heavy-based saucepan. Add the meat and cook quickly in small batches over medium heat until well browned. Drain on paper towels.

2 Return the meat to the pan and add the mustard, cream, wine, thyme and stock (broth). Bring to the boil, then reduce the heat and simmer, covered, for 1½ hours, stirring occasionally.

3 Add the mushrooms and cook for a further 15 minutes, or until the meat is tender. Delicious served with pasta and steamed vegetables.

CHILLI CON POLLO

Preparation time:
10 minutes

Total cooking time:
45 minutes

Serves 4

INGREDIENTS

- 1 tablespoon olive oil
- 1 onion, finely chopped
- 500 g (1 lb 2 oz) chicken mince (ground chicken)
- 1–2 teaspoons mild chilli powder
- 440 g (15½ oz) can chopped tomatoes
- 2 tablespoons tomato paste (tomato puree)
- 1–2 teaspoons soft brown sugar
- 425 g (15 oz) can red kidney beans, rinsed and drained

1 Heat the oil in a large saucepan. Add the chopped onion and cook over medium heat for 3 minutes, or until soft. Increase the heat to high and add the chicken mince (ground chicken). Cook until the chicken has browned, breaking up any lumps with a wooden spoon.

2 Add the chilli powder to the chicken and cook for 1 minute. Stir in the tomato, tomato paste (tomato puree) and ½ cup (125 ml/4¼ fl oz) water.

3 Bring to the boil, then reduce the heat and simmer for 30 minutes. Stir through the sugar to taste and the red kidney beans. Season. Serve with corn (nacho) chips or in taco shells with sour cream.

LAMB TAGINE

Preparation time:
15 minutes + 1 hour marinating

Total cooking time:
1 hour 45 minutes

Serves 6–8

INGREDIENTS

- 1.5 kg (3 lb 5 oz) leg or shoulder of lamb, cut into 2.5 cm (1 inch) pieces
- 3 cloves garlic, chopped
- ⅓ cup (80 ml/2¾ fl oz) olive oil
- 2 teaspoons ground cumin
- 1 teaspoon ground ginger
- 1 teaspoon ground turmeric
- 1 teaspoon paprika
- ½ teaspoon ground cinnamon
- 2 onions, thinly sliced
- 600 ml (20 fl oz) beef stock (broth)
- ¼ preserved lemon, pulp discarded, rind rinsed and cut into thin strips
- 425 g (15 oz) can chickpeas (garbanzo beans), drained
- 35 g (1¼ oz) cracked green olives
- ¼ cup (15 g/½ oz) chopped fresh coriander (cilantro) leaves

1 Place the lamb pieces in a non-metallic bowl, add the chopped garlic, 2 tablespoons of the olive oil and the ground cumin, ginger, turmeric, paprika, cinnamon, and ½ teaspoon ground black pepper and 1 teaspoon salt. Mix well to coat, then leave to marinate for 1 hour.

2 Heat the remaining olive oil in a large saucepan, add the lamb in batches and cook over high heat for 2–3 minutes, or until browned. Remove from the pan. Add the onion and cook for 2 minutes, then return the meat to the pan and add the beef stock (broth). Reduce the heat and simmer, covered, for 1 hour.

3 Add the preserved lemon strips, drained chickpeas (garbanzo beans) and olives, and cook, uncovered, for a further 30 minutes, or until the lamb is tender and the sauce has reduced and thickened. Stir in the coriander (cilantro). Serve in bowls with couscous.

SEAFOOD AND FENNEL STEW

Preparation time:	**Total cooking time:**	**Serves** 6
10 minutes	30 minutes	

INGREDIENTS

- 2 tablespoons olive oil
- 1 large fennel bulb, thinly sliced
- 2 leeks, thinly sliced
- 2 cloves garlic, crushed
- ½ teaspoon paprika
- 2 tablespoons anise-flavoured liqueur
- 200 ml (6¾ fl oz) dry white wine
- 18 mussels, scrubbed and beards removed

- ¼ teaspoon saffron threads
- ¼ teaspoon thyme leaves
- 6 baby octopus
- 16 raw prawns (shrimp), peeled and deveined
- 500 g (1 lb 2 oz) swordfish steaks, cut into large chunks
- 400 g (14 oz) baby new potatoes
- fennel greens, to garnish

1 Heat the oil in a large saucepan over medium heat. Add the fennel, leek and garlic. Stir in the paprika, season lightly and cook for 8 minutes, or until softened. Add the liqueur and wine, and stir for 1 minute, or until reduced by a third.

2 Add the mussels, discarding any open ones. Cover and cook for 1 minute, or until opened, discarding any that do not open. Remove from the pan to cool; remove from the shells and set aside.

3 Add the saffron and thyme to the pan, and cook for 1–2 minutes, stirring. Adjust the seasoning and transfer to a large, flameproof casserole dish.

4 Use a small sharp knife to remove the octopus heads. Grasp the bodies and push the beaks out with your index finger; remove and discard. Slit the heads and remove the gut. Mix the octopus, prawns (shrimp), fish and potatoes into the stew. Cover and cook gently for 10 minutes, or until tender. Add the mussels, cover and heat through. Garnish with fennel greens and serve.

CHICKEN WITH BALSAMIC VINEGAR

Preparation time:
5 minutes

Total cooking time:
50 minutes

Serves 4

INGREDIENTS

- 2 tablespoons olive oil
- 8 (1.2 kg/2 lb 10 oz) chicken pieces
- ½ cup (125 ml/4¼ fl oz) chicken stock (broth)
- ½ cup (125 ml/4¼ fl oz) dry white wine
- ½ cup (125 ml/4¼ fl oz) balsamic vinegar
- 40 g (1½ oz) chilled butter

1 Heat the oil in a large casserole dish over medium heat and cook the chicken, in batches, for 7–8 minutes, or until browned. Pour off any excess fat.

2 Add the stock (broth), bring to the boil, then reduce the heat and simmer, covered, for 30 minutes, or until the chicken is cooked through.

3 Add the white wine and vinegar and increase the heat to high. Boil for 1 minute, or until the liquid has thickened. Remove from the heat, stir in the butter until melted, and season. Spoon the sauce over the chicken to serve, accompanied by roast potatoes and salad.

NOTE: Use a good-quality balsamic vinegar, as the cheaper varieties can be too acidic.

DUCK WITH PEARS

Preparation time:
20 minutes

Total cooking time:
1 hour 40 minutes

Serves 4

INGREDIENTS

- 2 tablespoons olive oil
- 4 duck breasts
- 2 red onions, finely diced
- 1 carrot, finely diced
- 2 teaspoons fresh thyme
- 1 cup (250 ml / 8½ fl oz) chicken stock (broth)
- 2 ripe tomatoes, peeled, seeded and diced

- 4 green, firm pears, peeled, halved and cored (leaving the stems intact)
- 1 cinnamon stick
- 60 g (2 oz) blanched almonds, toasted, chopped
- 1 clove garlic
- 100 ml (3½ fl oz) brandy

1 Heat the oil in a heavy-based frying pan and cook the duck, skin-side down first, over medium heat until brown all over. Remove and set aside, reserving 4 tablespoons of the cooking fat.

2 Return 2 tablespoons of the fat to the pan. Add the onion, carrot and thyme, and cook over medium heat for 5 minutes, or until the onion has softened. Add the stock (broth) and tomato and bring to the boil. Reduce the heat and simmer for 30 minutes, with the lid slightly askew, or until the sauce has thickened and reduced. Cool slightly, then

puree in a food processor until smooth. Return to the pan with the duck. Simmer gently over low heat for 30–40 minutes, or until the duck is tender.

3 While the duck is cooking, place the pears in a saucepan with the cinnamon and just cover with cold water. Bring to the boil, reduce the heat and simmer gently for 5 minutes, or until the pears are tender but still firm. Remove the pears, cover to keep warm and add ½ cup (125 ml / 4¼ fl oz) of the pear poaching liquid to the tomato sauce.

4 Remove the duck from the sauce and keep warm. Grind the almonds, garlic and brandy together in a mortar and pestle or blender to make a smooth paste. Add to the tomato sauce, season, and cook for another 10 minutes.

5 Arrange the duck pieces on a serving plate and pour the sauce over the top. Arrange the warmed pears around the duck, and serve.

NOTE: The sauce adds an interesting finish to this Spanish dish, which is traditionally made with goose.

PORK AND LENTIL STEW

Preparation time:
20 minutes

Total cooking time:
1 hour

Serves 4

INGREDIENTS

- 1 tablespoon olive oil
- 2 onions, chopped
- 500 g (1 lb 2 oz) lean diced pork
- 2 teaspoons sweet Hungarian paprika
- 1 teaspoon hot paprika
- ½ teaspoon dried thyme
- 2 tablespoons tomato paste (tomato puree)
- 2 teaspoons soft brown sugar
- ¼ cup (60 g/2 oz) red lentils
- 1½ cups (375 ml/13 fl oz) beef stock (broth)
- 1 tomato
- 2 tablespoons low-fat plain yoghurt

1 Heat the olive oil in a large, deep saucepan over high heat. Add the onion, pork and paprikas, and stir for 3–4 minutes, or until browned.

2 Add the thyme, tomato paste (tomato puree), sugar, lentils, stock (broth), and salt and freshly ground black pepper. Bring to the boil, then reduce the heat to very low and cook, covered, for 20 minutes, stirring occasionally to prevent sticking. Uncover and cook for another 15–20 minutes, or until thickened.

3 Remove from the heat and set aside for 10 minutes. Cut the tomato in half and scoop out the seeds. Slice the flesh into thin strips.

4 Just before serving, stir the yoghurt into the stew. Scatter with the tomato strips and serve with rice, if desired.

BEEF POT ROAST

Preparation time:
15 minutes

Total cooking time:
3 hours 15 minutes

Serves 6

INGREDIENTS

- 300 g (10½ oz) baby brown onions
- 2 carrots
- 3 parsnips, peeled
- 40 g (1½ oz) butter
- 1–1.5 kg (2 lb 3 oz–3 lb 5 oz) eye of silverside (bottom round), trimmed of fat (see NOTE)
- ¼ cup (60 ml/2 fl oz) dry red wine
- 1 large tomato, finely chopped
- 1 cup (250 ml/8½ fl oz) beef stock (broth)
- mild or hot English mustard, to serve

1 Put the onions in a heatproof bowl and cover with boiling water. Leave for 1 minute, then drain well. Allow to cool, then peel off the skins.

2 Cut the carrots and parsnips in half lengthways, then into even-sized pieces. Heat half the butter in a large heavy-based saucepan that will tightly fit the meat (it will shrink during cooking), add the onions, carrot and parsnip, and cook, stirring, over medium–high heat until browned. Remove from the pan. Add the remaining butter to the pan and add the meat, browning well all over. Increase the heat to high and pour in the wine. Bring to the boil, then add the tomato and stock (broth). Return to the boil, then reduce the heat to low, cover and simmer for 2 hours, turning once. Add the vegetables and simmer, covered, for 1 hour.

3 Remove the meat from the pan and put it on a board ready for carving. Cover with foil and leave it to stand while finishing the sauce.

4 Increase the heat to high and boil the pan juices with the vegetables for 10 minutes to reduce and thicken slightly. Skim off any excess fat, and taste before seasoning. Slice the meat and arrange on a serving platter or individual serving plates with the vegetables. Drizzle generously with the pan juices. Serve with mustard.

NOTE: Eye of silverside (bottom round) is a tender, long-shaped cut of silverside that carves easily into serving-sized pieces. A regular piece of silverside (bottom round) or topside (top round) may be substituted.

POT ROAST PROVENÇALE

Preparation time:
15 minutes

Total cooking time:
2 hours 15 minutes

Serves 6

INGREDIENTS

- 2 tablespoons oil
- 2 kg (4 lb) rolled beef brisket, trimmed
- 3 cups (750 ml/26 fl oz) beef stock (broth)
- 1 cup (250 ml/8½ fl oz) red wine
- ¼ cup (60 ml/2 fl oz) brandy
- 2 onions, quartered
- 3 cloves garlic, crushed
- 3 tomatoes, peeled, seeded and chopped
- 2 bay leaves
- ¼ cup (15 g/½ oz) chopped fresh parsley
- 2 tablespoons fresh thyme leaves
- 12 pitted black (ripe) olives
- 6 small carrots, thickly sliced
- 2 tablespoons plain (all-purpose) flour

1 Heat the oil in a deep heavy-based saucepan. Cook the meat over medium–high heat until browned all over, then remove from the heat.

2 Add the stock (broth) to the pan with the wine, brandy, onion, garlic, tomato, bay leaves, parsley and thyme. Cover and bring to simmering point over low heat. Simmer for 1½ hours.

3 Add the olives and carrot, and cook for 30 minutes. Remove the meat and leave it in a warm place, covered with foil, for 10 minutes before slicing.

4 Combine the flour and ¼ cup (60 ml/2 fl oz) water to make a smooth paste. Add to the sauce, stir over medium heat until the sauce thickens, and cook for 3 minutes. Pour over the sliced meat to serve.

SPICY APRICOT CHICKEN

Preparation time:
10 minutes

Total cooking time:
20 minutes

Serves 4

INGREDIENTS

- 750 g (1 lb 10 oz) chicken thigh fillets, cut into 5 cm (2 inch) pieces
- plain (all-purpose) flour, for coating
- 2 tablespoons oil
- 2 teaspoons red curry paste
- 2 spring (green) onions, sliced
- 415 g (14⅔ oz) can apricot halves in light syrup
- ½ cup (125 ml/4¼ fl oz) chicken stock (broth)
- 200 g (7 oz) plain yoghurt
- 2 tablespoons chopped fresh coriander (cilantro) leaves
- fresh coriander (cilantro) leaves, extra, to garnish

1 Lightly coat the chicken in the flour. Heat the oil in a saucepan, add the curry paste and stir over low heat for 1 minute. Add the spring (green) onion and chicken, and cook, stirring, over medium heat for 2–3 minutes, or until the chicken is golden.

2 Drain the apricots and reserve ½ cup (125 ml/4¼ fl oz) apricot juice. Add the reserved juice, apricots and stock (broth) to the pan. Bring to the boil, then reduce the heat and simmer for 10 minutes, or until the chicken is tender.

3 Mix together the yoghurt and coriander (cilantro), and place a spoonful of the mixture over each serving of chicken. Garnish with extra coriander (cilantro) leaves. Serve with couscous or rice.

BEEF STROGANOFF

Preparation time:
25 minutes

Total cooking time:
30 minutes

Serves 6

INGREDIENTS

- 1 kg (2 lb 3 oz) piece rump (round or boneless sirloin) steak, trimmed
- ⅓ cup (40 g/1½ oz) plain (all-purpose) flour
- ¼ teaspoon ground black pepper
- ¼ cup (60 ml/2 fl oz) olive oil
- 1 large onion, chopped
- 500 g (1 lb 2 oz) baby mushrooms
- 1 tablespoon sweet paprika
- 1 tablespoon tomato paste (tomato puree)
- 2 teaspoons French mustard
- ½ cup (125 ml/4¼ fl oz) dry white wine
- ¼ cup (60 ml/2 fl oz) chicken stock (broth)
- ¾ cup (185 g/6½ oz) sour cream
- 1 tablespoon finely chopped fresh parsley

1 Slice the meat across the grain into short, thin pieces. Combine the flour and pepper. Toss the meat in the seasoned flour, shaking off the excess.

2 Heat 2 tablespoons of the oil in a heavy-based saucepan. Cook the meat quickly in small batches over medium–high heat until well browned. Drain on paper towels.

3 Heat the remaining oil in the pan. Cook the onion over medium heat for 3 minutes, or until soft. Add the mushrooms and stir for 5 minutes.

4 Add the paprika, tomato paste (tomato puree), mustard, wine and stock (broth) to the pan, and bring to the boil. Reduce the heat and simmer for 5 minutes, uncovered, stirring occasionally. Return the meat to the pan with the sour cream, and stir until combined and just heated through. Sprinkle with the parsley just before serving.

BEEF AND LENTIL CURRY

Preparation time:
45 minutes +
10 minutes soaking

Total cooking time:
1 hour 50 minutes

Serves 6

INGREDIENTS

- 3–4 small dried red chillies
- ¼ cup (60 ml/2 fl oz) oil
- 2 red onions, cut into thin wedges
- 4 cloves garlic, finely chopped
- 1 tablespoon grated fresh ginger (gingerroot)
- 1 tablespoon garam masala
- 3 cardamom pods, lightly crushed
- 1 cinnamon stick
- 2 teaspoons ground turmeric
- 750 g (1 lb 10 oz) chuck or gravy (boneless shin) beef, diced
- 400 g (14 oz) can chopped tomatoes

- ½ cup (95 g/3⅓ oz) brown or green lentils
- ½ cup (125 g/4⅓ oz) red lentils
- 200 g (7 oz) pumpkin, diced
- 150 g (5¼ oz) baby eggplant (aubergine), quartered lengthways, diced
- 125 g (4⅓ oz) baby English (common) spinach
- 1 tablespoon tamarind puree
- 2 tablespoons grated palm sugar or soft brown sugar

1 Soak the chillies in boiling water for 10 minutes, then drain and finely chop.

2 Heat the oil in a large saucepan. Add the onion and cook, stirring, over medium heat for 5 minutes, or until soft. Add the garlic and ginger (gingerroot), and cook for a further 2 minutes.

3 Add the chopped chilli, garam masala, cardamom pods, cinnamon stick, turmeric and ½ teaspoon coarsely ground black pepper. Cook, stirring, for 2 minutes, or until fragrant. Add the beef and stir constantly for 3–4 minutes, or until the meat changes colour and is well coated in the spices.

4 Add the tomato, lentils,
1 teaspoon salt and 3 cups
(750 ml / 26 fl oz) water. Simmer,
covered, for 1 hour, or until the
lentils are tender. Stir frequently
to prevent any of the mixture
sticking to the base of the
pan. Add a little extra water,
if necessary.

5 Add the pumpkin and eggplant
(aubergine) to the pan, and cook,
covered, for 20 minutes, or until

the beef and vegetables are
tender and the sauce thickens.
Stir in the spinach, tamarind
puree and palm sugar, and
cook, covered, for a further
10 minutes. Remove the
cinnamon stick, and serve.

NOTE: This dish is traditionally
served with rice that has been
cooked pilaff-style with well-
browned, slow-cooked onion
slices.

CHICKEN KAPITAN

Preparation time:
35 minutes

Total cooking time:
1 hour 20 minutes

Serves 4–6

INGREDIENTS

- 1 teaspoon small dried shrimp
- ⅓ cup (80 ml/2¾ fl oz) oil
- 6–8 fresh red chillies, seeded and finely chopped
- 4 cloves garlic, finely chopped
- 3 stems lemongrass (white part only), finely chopped
- 2 teaspoons ground turmeric
- 10 candlenuts
- 2 large onions, chopped
- 1 cup (250 ml/8½ fl oz) coconut milk
- 1.5 kg (3 lb 5 oz) chicken, cut into 8 pieces
- ½ cup (125 ml/4¼ fl oz) coconut cream
- 2 tablespoons lime juice

1 Put the shrimp in a frying pan and dry-fry over low heat, shaking the pan regularly, for 3 minutes, or until the shrimp are dark orange and are giving off a strong aroma. Transfer to a mortar and pestle, and pound until finely ground. Alternatively, process in a food processor.

2 Place half the oil, the chilli, garlic, lemongrass, turmeric and candlenuts in a food processor, and process in short bursts until very finely chopped, regularly scraping down the side of the bowl.

3 Heat the remaining oil in a wok or frying pan, add the onion and ¼ teaspoon salt, and cook, stirring regularly, over low heat for 8 minutes, or until golden.

4 Add the spice mixture and shrimp, and stir for 5 minutes. If the mixture begins to stick, add 2 tablespoons of the coconut milk. It is important to cook the mixture thoroughly to develop the flavours.

5 Add the chicken to the wok and cook, stirring, for 5 minutes, or until beginning to brown. Stir in the remaining coconut milk and 1 cup (250 ml/8½ fl oz) water, and bring to the boil. Reduce the heat and simmer for 50 minutes, or until the chicken is cooked and the sauce has thickened slightly. Add the coconut cream and bring the mixture back to the boil, stirring constantly. Add the lime juice and serve immediately with rice.

SEAFOOD AND TOFU CURRY

Preparation time:
30 minutes

Total cooking time:
30 minutes

Serves 4

INGREDIENTS

- 2 tablespoons soy bean oil, or oil
- 500 g (1 lb 2 oz) firm white fish (ling, perch), cut into 2 cm (¾ inch) cubes
- 250 g (8¾ oz) raw prawns (shrimp), peeled and deveined, tails intact
- 2 × 400 ml (13½ fl oz) cans coconut milk
- 1 tablespoon red curry paste
- 4 fresh or 8 dried kaffir lime leaves
- 2 tablespoons fish sauce
- 2 tablespoons finely chopped fresh lemongrass (white part only)
- 2 cloves garlic, crushed

- 1 tablespoon finely chopped fresh galangal
- 1 tablespoon shaved palm sugar or soft brown sugar
- 300 g (10½ oz) silken firm tofu, cut into 1.5 cm (⅝ inch) cubes
- ½ cup (125 g/4⅓ oz) bamboo shoots, julienned
- 1 large fresh red chilli, thinly sliced
- 2 teaspoons lime juice
- spring (green) onions, chopped, to garnish
- fresh coriander (cilantro) leaves, chopped, to garnish

1 Heat the oil in a large frying pan or wok over medium heat. Sear the fish and prawns (shrimp) for 1 minute on each side. Remove the fish and prawns (shrimp) from the pan.

2 Place ¼ cup (60 ml/2 fl oz) of the coconut milk and the curry paste in the pan, and cook over medium heat for 2 minutes, or until fragrant and the oil separates. Add the remaining coconut milk, kaffir lime leaves, fish sauce, lemongrass, garlic, galangal, palm sugar and 1 teaspoon salt. Cook over low heat for 15 minutes.

3 Add the tofu cubes, bamboo shoots and sliced chilli. Simmer for a further 3–5 minutes. Return to medium heat, add the seafood and lime juice, and cook for a further 3 minutes, or until the seafood is just cooked. Remove from the heat.

4 Serve the curry with steamed rice and garnish with the spring (green) onion and coriander (cilantro) leaves.

PANANG BEEF

Preparation time:
30 minutes + 5 minutes soaking

Total cooking time:
1 hour 30 minutes

Serves 4–6

INGREDIENTS

CURRY PASTE
- 8–10 large dried red chillies
- 6 red Asian shallots, chopped
- 6 cloves garlic, chopped
- 1 teaspoon ground coriander
- 1 tablespoon ground cumin
- 1 teaspoon white pepper
- 2 stems lemongrass (white part only), bruised and sliced
- 1 tablespoon chopped fresh galangal
- 6 coriander (cilantro) roots
- 2 teaspoons shrimp paste
- 2 tablespoons roasted peanuts
- peanut oil, if needed
- 1 tablespoon peanut oil

- 400 ml (13½ fl oz) can coconut cream (do not shake the can – see NOTE)
- 1 kg (2 lb 3 oz) rump (round or boneless sirloin) or blade steak, thinly sliced
- 400 ml (13½ fl oz) can coconut milk
- 4 kaffir lime leaves, whole
- ⅓ cup (90 g/3¼ oz) crunchy peanut butter
- ¼ cup (60 ml/2 fl oz) lime juice
- 2½ tablespoons fish sauce
- 3–4 tablespoons palm sugar or soft brown sugar
- fresh Thai basil leaves, to garnish
- 1 tablespoon chopped peanuts, extra, to garnish (optional)

1 To make the curry paste, soak the chillies in boiling water for 5 minutes, or until soft. Remove the stem and seeds, then chop. Place all the curry paste ingredients in a food processor and process to a smooth paste. Add a little peanut oil if it is too thick.

2 Place the oil and the thick cream from the top of the coconut cream (reserving the rest) in a large saucepan over high heat. Add 6–8 tablespoons of the curry paste and cook, stirring, for 5 minutes, or until fragrant. Cook for 5–10 minutes, or until the coconut cream splits and becomes oily.

3 Add the beef, the reserved coconut cream, coconut milk, lime leaves and peanut butter, and cook for 8 minutes, or until the beef just starts to change colour. Reduce the heat and simmer for 1 hour, or until the beef is tender.

4 Stir in the lime juice, fish sauce and palm sugar, and transfer to a serving dish. Garnish with the Thai basil leaves, and extra peanuts, if desired, and serve immediately.

NOTE: Do not shake the can of coconut cream because good-quality coconut cream has a layer of very thick cream at the top that has separated from the rest of the cream. This has a higher fat content, which causes it to split or separate more readily than the rest of the coconut cream or milk.

PORK VINDALOO

Preparation time:
20 minutes

Total cooking time:
2 hours

Serves 4

INGREDIENTS

- ¼ cup (60 ml/2 fl oz) oil
- 1 kg (2 lb 3 oz) pork fillets, cut into bite-size pieces
- 2 onions, finely chopped
- 4 cloves garlic, finely chopped
- 1 tablespoon finely chopped fresh ginger (gingerroot)
- 1 tablespoon garam masala
- 2 teaspoons brown mustard seeds
- 4 tablespoons vindaloo paste

1 Heat the oil in a saucepan, add the pork in small batches and cook over medium heat for 5–7 minutes, or until browned. Remove from the pan.

2 Add the onion, garlic, ginger (gingerroot), garam masala and mustard seeds to the pan, and cook, stirring, for 5 minutes, or until the onion is soft.

3 Return all the meat to the pan, add the vindaloo paste and cook, stirring, for 2 minutes. Add 2½ cups (625 ml/21 fl oz) water and bring to the boil. Reduce the heat and simmer, covered, for 1½ hours, or until the meat is tender. Serve with boiled rice and pappadums.

LAMB KORMA

Preparation time:
30 minutes + 1 hour marinating

Total cooking time:
1 hour 10 minutes

Serves 4–6

INGREDIENTS

- 2 kg (4 lb 7 oz) leg of lamb, boned
- 1 onion, chopped
- 2 teaspoons grated fresh ginger (gingerroot)
- 3 cloves garlic
- 2 teaspoons ground coriander
- 2 teaspoons ground cumin
- 1 teaspoon cardamom seeds
- large pinch cayenne (red) pepper
- 2 tablespoons ghee or oil
- 1 onion, extra, sliced
- 2½ tablespoons tomato paste (tomato puree)
- ½ cup (125 g/4⅓ oz) plain yoghurt
- ½ cup (125 ml/4¼ fl oz) coconut cream
- ½ cup (50 g/1¼ oz) ground almonds
- toasted slivered almonds, to serve

1 Trim any excess fat or sinew from the lamb, cut it into 3 cm (1¼ inch) cubes and place in a large bowl.

2 Place the chopped onion, grated ginger (gingerroot), garlic, ground coriander, ground cumin, cardamom seeds, cayenne (red) pepper and ½ teaspoon salt in a food processor. Process the ingredients until they form a smooth paste. Add the spice mixture to a large bowl with the cubed lamb and mix well to coat the lamb in the spice mixture. Leave to marinate for 1 hour.

3 Heat the ghee or oil in a large saucepan, add the sliced onion and cook, stirring, over low heat for 7 minutes, or until the onion is soft. Add the lamb and spice mixture, and cook, stirring constantly, for 8–10 minutes, or until the lamb changes colour. Stir in the tomato paste, yoghurt, coconut cream and ground almonds.

4 Reduce the heat and simmer the curry, covered, stirring occasionally, for 50 minutes, or until the meat is tender. Add a little water if the mixture becomes too dry. Season the curry with salt and pepper, and garnish with the toasted slivered almonds. Serve with steamed rice.

NOTE: Korma curries can also be made using beef or chicken. Korma refers to the style of curry – rich and smooth, and including almonds.

GREEN CHICKEN CURRY

Preparation time:
40 minutes

Total cooking time:
30 minutes

Serves 4–6

INGREDIENTS

- 2 cups (500 ml/17 fl oz) coconut cream (do not shake the can)
- 4 tablespoons green curry paste
- 2 tablespoons grated palm sugar or soft brown sugar
- 2 tablespoons fish sauce
- 4 kaffir lime leaves, finely shredded
- 1 kg (2 lb 3 oz) chicken thigh or breast fillets, cut into thick strips
- 200 g (7 oz) bamboo shoots, cut into thick strips
- 100 g (3½ oz) snake beans, cut into 5 cm (2 inch) lengths
- ½ cup (15 g/½ oz) fresh Thai basil leaves

1 Place ½ cup (125 ml/4¼ fl oz) of the thick coconut cream from the top of the can in a wok, and bring to the boil. Add the curry paste, then reduce the heat and simmer for 15 minutes, or until fragrant and the oil starts to separate from the cream. Add the palm sugar, fish sauce and kaffir lime leaves to the pan.

2 Stir in the remaining coconut cream and the chicken, bamboo shoots and beans, and simmer for 15 minutes, or until the chicken is tender. Stir in the Thai basil and serve with rice.

THAI BEEF CURRY

Preparation time:
20 minutes

Total cooking time:
1 hour 30 minutes

Serves 6

INGREDIENTS

- 2 tablespoons oil
- 750 g (1 lb 10 oz) blade steak, thinly sliced
- 4 tablespoons Musaman curry paste
- 2 cloves garlic, finely chopped
- 1 onion, sliced lengthways
- 6 curry leaves, torn
- 3 cups (750 ml/26 fl oz) coconut milk
- 450 g (14 oz) butternut pumpkin (squash), roughly diced
- 2 tablespoons chopped unsalted peanuts
- 1 tablespoon palm sugar or soft brown sugar
- 2 tablespoons tamarind puree
- 2 tablespoons fish sauce
- curry leaves, extra, to garnish

1 Heat a wok or frying pan over high heat. Add the oil and swirl to coat the side. Add the meat in batches and cook for 5 minutes, or until browned. Remove the meat from the wok.

2 Add the curry paste, garlic, onion and curry leaves to the wok, and stir to coat. Return the meat to the wok and cook, stirring, over medium heat for 2 minutes.

3 Add the coconut milk to the wok, then reduce the heat and simmer for 45 minutes. Add the diced pumpkin (squash) and simmer for 25–30 minutes, or until the meat and the vegetables are tender and the sauce has thickened.

4 Stir in the peanuts, palm sugar, tamarind puree and fish sauce, and simmer for 1 minute. Garnish with curry leaves. Serve with steamed rice.

DUCK AND COCONUT CURRY

Preparation time:
20 minutes

Total cooking time:
1 hour 15 minutes

Serves 6

INGREDIENTS

CURRY PASTE
- 1 red onion, chopped
- 2 cloves garlic
- 2 coriander (cilantro) roots, chopped
- 2 teaspoons chopped fresh ginger (gingerroot)
- 1½ teaspoons coriander seeds, dry-roasted and ground
- 1 teaspoon cardamom seeds, dry-roasted and ground
- 1 teaspoon fenugreek seeds, dry-roasted and ground

- 1 teaspoon brown mustard seeds, dry-roasted and ground
- 10 black peppercorns, ground
- 2 teaspoons garam masala
- ¼ teaspoon ground turmeric
- 2 teaspoons tamarind puree
- 6–8 duck breast fillets
- 1 red onion, sliced
- ½ cup (125 ml/4¼ fl oz) white vinegar
- 2 cups (500 ml/17 fl oz) coconut milk
- 2 tablespoons fresh coriander (cilantro) leaves

1 To make the curry paste, place all the ingredients in a food processor and process to a thick paste.

2 Trim any excess fat from the duck fillets, then place, skin-side down, in a large saucepan and cook over medium heat for 10 minutes, or until the skin is brown and any remaining fat has melted. Turn the fillets over and cook for 5 minutes, or until tender. Remove and drain on paper towels.

3 Reserve 1 tablespoon duck fat, discarding the remaining fat. Add the onion and cook for 5 minutes, then add the curry paste and stir over low heat for 10 minutes, or until fragrant.

4 Return the duck to the pan and
 stir to coat with the paste. Stir
 in the vinegar, coconut milk,
 1 teaspoon salt and ½ cup
 (125 ml/4¼ fl oz) water. Simmer,
covered, for 45 minutes, or until
the fillets are tender. Stir in the
coriander (cilantro) leaves just
prior to serving. Serve with rice
and naan bread.

GOAN FISH CURRY

Preparation time:
20 minutes

Total cooking time:
35 minutes

Serves 6

INGREDIENTS

- ¼ cup (60 ml/2 fl oz) oil
- 1 large onion, finely chopped
- 4–5 cloves garlic, chopped
- 2 teaspoons grated fresh ginger (gingerroot)
- 4–6 small dried red chillies
- 1 tablespoon coriander seeds
- 2 teaspoons cumin seeds
- 1 teaspoon ground turmeric
- ¼ teaspoon chilli powder

- ⅓ cup (30 g/1 oz) desiccated (fine) coconut
- 270 ml (9¼ fl oz) coconut milk
- 2 tomatoes, peeled and chopped
- 2 tablespoons tamarind puree
- 1 tablespoon white vinegar
- 6 curry leaves
- 1 kg (2 lb 3 oz) boneless, skinless firm fish fillets, such as flake or ling, cut into 8 cm (3 inch) pieces

1 Heat the oil in a large saucepan. Add the onion and cook, stirring, over low heat for 10 minutes, or until softened and lightly golden. Add the garlic and ginger (gingerroot), and cook for a further 2 minutes.

2 Meanwhile, place the dried chillies, coriander seeds, cumin seeds, turmeric, chilli powder and coconut in a frying pan, and dry-fry, stirring constantly, over medium heat for 2 minutes, or

until the mixture is aromatic. Place in a food processor or spice grinder and finely grind.

3 Add the spice mixture, coconut milk, chopped tomato, tamarind puree, vinegar and curry leaves to the onion mixture. Stir to mix thoroughly, add 1 cup (250 ml/8½ fl oz) water and simmer for 10 minutes, or until the tomato has softened and the mixture has thickened slightly. Stir frequently to prevent sticking.

4 Add the fish and cook, covered, over low heat for 10 minutes, or until cooked through. Stir gently once or twice during cooking and add a little water if the mixture is too thick. Serve immediately with rice and pappadums.

LAMB AND SPINACH CURRY

Preparation time:
30 minutes

Total cooking time:
2 hours 20 minutes

Serves 6

INGREDIENTS

- 1 kg (2 lb 3 oz) English (common) spinach
- ½ cup (125 ml/4¼ fl oz) oil
- 1.5 kg (3 lb 5 oz) lamb, cut into 3 cm (1¼ inch) cubes (see NOTE)
- 2 red onions, finely chopped
- 6 cloves garlic, crushed
- 1½ tablespoons grated fresh ginger (gingerroot)
- 2 bay leaves

- 2 tablespoons ground coriander
- 1 tablespoon ground cumin
- 1 teaspoon ground turmeric
- 2 large vine-ripened tomatoes, peeled, seeded and chopped
- 2–3 small fresh green chillies, seeded and finely chopped
- 100 g (3½ oz) plain thick yoghurt
- 1 cinnamon stick
- 2 teaspoons garam masala

---

1 Preheat the oven to warm 170°C (340°F/Gas 3). Trim the spinach and quickly blanch in simmering water. Drain, cool slightly and squeeze to remove any excess moisture, then place in a food processor and process until smooth.

2 Heat half the oil in a large saucepan. Add the lamb pieces in batches and cook over high heat for 4–5 minutes, or until browned. Remove the lamb from the pan.

3 Heat the remaining oil in the saucepan. Add the onion and cook, stirring frequently, for 10 minutes, or until golden brown but not burnt. Add the garlic, ginger (gingerroot) and bay leaves, and cook, stirring, for 3 more minutes.

4 Add the spices and cook, stirring, for 2 minutes, or until fragrant. Add the tomato and chilli, and stir over low heat for 5 minutes, or until the tomato is thick and pulpy. Remove from the heat and cool for 5 minutes. Transfer to a 4 litre (4.2 US qt/ 3.5 UK qt) casserole dish and stir in the yoghurt.

5 Return the meat to the dish and add the cinnamon stick and 1 teaspoon salt. Bake, covered, for 1 hour and then uncovered for a further 15 minutes. Stir in the spinach and garam masala, and cook, stirring occasionally, for 15 minutes, or until the meat is tender. Remove the bay leaves and cinnamon stick, and serve with rice or pilaf.

NOTE: Ask your butcher to bone and cut the lamb for you. A 2.2 kg (4 lb 14 oz) leg will yield about 1.5 kg (3 lb 5 oz) meat.

RED BEEF CURRY

Preparation time:
40 minutes

Total cooking time:
1 hour 30 minutes

Serves 4

INGREDIENTS

- 1 cup (250 ml/8½ fl oz) coconut cream (do not shake the can)
- 2 tablespoons red curry paste
- 500 g (1 lb 2 oz) rump (round or boneless sirloin) or topside steak, cut into strips (see NOTE)
- 2 tablespoons fish sauce
- 1 tablespoon palm sugar or soft brown sugar
- 5 kaffir lime leaves, halved
- 2 cups (500 ml/17 fl oz) coconut milk
- 8 Thai eggplants (aubergines), halved
- 2 tablespoons finely shredded fresh Thai basil leaves

1 Place the thick coconut cream from the top of the can in a wok and bring to the boil. Boil for 10 minutes, or until the oil starts to separate. Add the curry paste and simmer, stirring to prevent it sticking to the bottom, for 5 minutes, or until fragrant.

2 Add the meat and cook, stirring, for 3–5 minutes, or until it changes colour. Add the fish sauce, palm sugar, lime leaves, coconut milk and remaining coconut cream, and simmer for 1 hour, or until the meat is tender and the sauce has slightly thickened.

3 Add the eggplant (aubergine) and cook for 10 minutes, or until tender. If the sauce is too thick, add a little water. Stir in half the shredded basil leaves. Garnish with the remaining basil leaves and serve with rice.

NOTE: Cut the meat into 5 × 5 × 2 cm (2 × 2 × ¾ inch) pieces, then cut across the grain at a 45° angle into 5 mm (¼ inch) thick slices.

MUSAMAN BEEF CURRY

Preparation time:
30 minutes

Total cooking time:
1 hour 45 minutes

Serves 4

INGREDIENTS

- 1 tablespoon tamarind pulp
- 2 tablespoons oil
- 750 g (1 lb 10 oz) lean stewing beef, cubed
- 2 cups (500 ml/17 fl oz) coconut milk
- 4 cardamom pods, bruised
- 2 cups (500 ml/17 fl oz) coconut cream
- 2–3 tablespoons Musaman curry paste
- 8 baby onions, peeled (see NOTE)
- 8 baby potatoes, peeled (see NOTE)
- 2 tablespoons fish sauce
- 2 tablespoons palm sugar or soft brown sugar
- ½ cup (80 g/2¾ oz) unsalted peanuts, roasted and ground
- fresh coriander (cilantro) leaves, to garnish

1 Place the tamarind pulp and ½ cup (125 ml/4¼ fl oz) boiling water in a bowl and set aside to cool. When cool, mash the pulp to dissolve in the water, then strain and reserve the liquid. Discard the pulp.

2 Heat the oil in a wok or a large saucepan and cook the beef in batches over high heat for 5 minutes, or until browned. Reduce the heat, add the coconut milk and cardamom, and simmer for 1 hour, or until the beef is tender. Remove the beef, strain and reserve the beef and cooking liquid.

3 Heat the coconut cream in the wok and stir in the curry paste. Cook for 5 minutes, or until the oil starts to separate from the cream.

4 Add the onions, potatoes, fish sauce, palm sugar, peanuts, beef mixture, reserved cooking liquid and tamarind water, and simmer for 25–30 minutes. Garnish with fresh coriander (cilantro) leaves. Serve with rice.

NOTE: Use small onions and potatoes, about 25–30 g (¾–1 oz) each.

LAMB NECK CURRY

Preparation time:
30 minutes

Total cooking time:
1 hour 35 minutes

Serves 4–6

INGREDIENTS

- 1 tablespoon oil
- 8 best lamb neck chops (see NOTE)
- 2 onions, sliced
- 3 cloves garlic, finely chopped
- 2 teaspoons finely chopped fresh ginger (gingerroot)
- 1 small fresh green chilli, seeded and finely chopped
- ½ teaspoon ground cumin
- 1 teaspoon ground fennel
- 1½ teaspoons ground turmeric
- 1½ teaspoons chilli powder
- 2 teaspoons garam masala
- 1 star anise
- 1 cinnamon stick
- 5 curry leaves
- 2 bay leaves
- 2 cups (500 ml/17 fl oz) beef stock (broth)
- 8 tomatoes, peeled and quartered

1 Heat the oil in a large frying pan and cook the lamb in batches for 5–8 minutes, or until browned. Place the chops in a large saucepan.

2 Add the onion to the frying pan and cook, stirring frequently, for 5 minutes, or until soft and browned. Stir in the garlic, ginger (gingerroot) and chilli, and cook for 1 minute. Then stir in the cumin, fennel, turmeric, chilli powder, garam masala, star anise, cinnamon stick, curry leaves and bay leaves, and cook, stirring to prevent sticking, for a further 1 minute.

3 Add 2 tablespoons cold water to the frying pan, mix well, and then add the beef stock (broth). Bring to the boil, then pour over the lamb. Stir in the tomato, reduce the heat and simmer, covered, for 1¼ hours. Serve with jasmine rice tossed with coriander (cilantro).

NOTE: Best lamb neck chops come from the meat just under the shoulder and are sweeter, leaner and meatier than lamb neck.

CHICKEN CURRY WITH APRICOTS

Preparation time:
40 minutes + 1 hour
soaking

Total cooking time:
1 hour 10 minutes

Serves 6–8

INGREDIENTS

- 18 dried apricots
- 1 tablespoon ghee or oil
- 2 × 1.5 kg (3 lb 5 oz) chickens, jointed
- 3 onions, thinly sliced
- 1 teaspoon grated fresh ginger (gingerroot)
- 3 cloves garlic, crushed

- 3 large fresh green chillies, seeded and finely chopped
- 1 teaspoon cumin seeds
- 1 teaspoon chilli powder
- ½ teaspoon ground turmeric
- 4 cardamom pods, bruised
- 4 large tomatoes, peeled and cut into eighths

1 Soak the dried apricots in 1 cup (250 ml/8½ fl oz) hot water for 1 hour.

2 Melt the ghee or oil in a large saucepan, add the chicken in batches and cook over high heat for 5–6 minutes, or until browned. Remove from the pan. Add the onion and cook, stirring often, for 10 minutes, or until the onion has softened and turned golden brown.

3 Add the ginger (gingerroot), garlic and chopped green chilli, and cook, stirring, for 2 minutes. Stir in the cumin seeds, chilli powder and ground turmeric, and cook for a further 1 minute.

4 Return the chicken to the pan, add the cardamom, tomato and apricots, with any remaining liquid, and mix well. Simmer, covered, for 35 minutes, or until the chicken is tender.

5 Remove the chicken, cover and keep warm. Bring the liquid to the boil and boil rapidly, uncovered, for 5 minutes, or until it has thickened slightly.

To serve, spoon the liquid over the chicken. Serve with steamed rice mixed with raisins (dark raisins), grated carrot and toasted flaked almonds.

BALTI CHICKEN

Preparation time:
25 minutes

Total cooking time:
1 hour

Serves 6

INGREDIENTS

- 1 kg (2 lb 3 oz) chicken thigh fillets
- ⅓ cup (80 ml/2¾ fl oz) oil
- 1 large red onion, finely chopped
- 4–5 cloves garlic, finely chopped
- 1 tablespoon grated fresh ginger (gingerroot)
- 2 teaspoons ground cumin
- 2 teaspoons ground coriander
- 1 teaspoon ground turmeric
- ½ teaspoon chilli powder

- 425 g (15 oz) can chopped tomatoes
- 1 green capsicum (pepper), cut into 3 cm (1¼ inch) cubes
- 1–2 small fresh green chillies, seeded and finely chopped
- ⅓ cup (20 g/⅔ oz) chopped fresh coriander (cilantro)
- 2 chopped spring (green) onions, to garnish

1 Remove any excess fat or sinew from the chicken thigh fillets and cut into 4–5 pieces.

2 Heat a large wok over high heat, add the oil and swirl to coat the side. Add the onion and stir-fry (scramble-fry) over medium heat for 5 minutes, or until softened but not browned. Add the garlic and ginger (gingerroot), and stir-fry for 3 minutes.

3 Add the spices, 1 teaspoon salt and ¼ cup (60 ml/2 fl oz) water. Increase the heat to high and stir-fry (scramble-fry) for 2 minutes, or until the mixture has thickened. Take care not to burn.

4 Add the tomato and 1 cup (250 ml/8½ fl oz) water and cook, stirring often, for a further 10 minutes, or until the mixture is thick and pulpy and the oil comes to the surface.

5 Add the chicken to the wok, reduce the heat and simmer, stirring often, for 15 minutes. Add the capsicum (pepper) and chilli, and simmer for 25 minutes, or until the chicken is tender. Add a little water if the mixture is too thick. Stir in the coriander (cilantro) and garnish with the spring (green) onion. Serve with rice.

NOTE: This curry is traditionally cooked in a Karahi or Balti pan, which is a round-bottomed, cast-iron, two-handled dish. A wok makes a good substitute.

BEEF RENDANG

Preparation time:
20 minutes

Total cooking time:
2 hours 30 minutes

Serves 6

INGREDIENTS

- 2 onions, roughly chopped
- 2 cloves garlic, crushed
- 400 ml (13½ fl oz) can coconut milk
- 2 teaspoons ground coriander seeds
- ½ teaspoon ground fennel seeds
- 2 teaspoons ground cumin seeds
- ¼ teaspoon ground cloves
- 1.5 kg (3 lb 5 oz) chuck steak, cut into 3 cm (1¼ inch) cubes
- 4–6 small fresh red chillies, chopped
- 1 tablespoon lemon juice
- 1 stem lemongrass (white part only), bruised, cut lengthways
- 2 teaspoons grated palm sugar or soft brown sugar

1 Place the onion and garlic in a food processor, and process until smooth, adding water, if necessary.

2 Place the coconut milk in a large saucepan and bring to the boil, then reduce the heat to medium and cook, stirring occasionally, for 15 minutes, or until the milk has reduced by half and the oil has separated. Do not allow the milk to brown.

3 Add the coriander, fennel, cumin and cloves to the pan, and stir for 1 minute. Add the meat and cook for 2 minutes, or until it changes colour. Add the onion mixture, chilli, lemon juice, lemongrass and sugar. Cook, covered, over medium heat for 2 hours, or until the liquid has reduced and the mixture has thickened. Stir frequently to prevent it sticking to the bottom of the pan.

4 Uncover and continue cooking until the oil from the coconut milk begins to emerge again, letting the curry develop colour and flavour. Be careful that it does not burn. The curry is cooked when it is brown and dry.

MADRAS BEEF CURRY

Preparation time:
20 minutes

Total cooking time:
1 hour 45 minutes

Serves 4

INGREDIENTS

* 1 tablespoon oil or ghee
* 1 onion, chopped
* 3–4 tablespoons Madras curry paste
* 1 kg (2 lb 3 oz) skirt or chuck steak, cut into 2.5 cm (1 inch) cubes
* ¼ cup (60 g/2 oz) tomato paste (tomato puree)
* 1 cup (250 ml/8½ fl oz) beef stock (broth)

1 Heat the oil in a large frying pan, add the onion and cook over medium heat for 10 minutes, or until browned. Add the curry paste and stir for 1 minute, or until fragrant. Then add the meat and cook, stirring, until coated with the curry paste.

2 Stir in the tomato paste (tomato puree) and stock (broth). Reduce the heat and simmer, covered, for 1¼ hours, and then uncovered for 15 minutes, or until the meat is tender.

VIETNAMESE CHICKEN CURRY

Preparation time:
30 minutes + overnight refrigeration

Total cooking time:
1 hour 10 minutes

Serves 6

INGREDIENTS

- 4 large chicken Marylands (leg and thigh pieces)
- 1 tablespoon good-quality Indian curry powder
- 1 teaspoon caster (berry) sugar
- ⅓ cup (80 ml/2¾ fl oz) oil
- 500 g (1 lb 2 oz) orange sweet potato (yam), cut into 3 cm (1¼ inch) cubes
- 1 large onion, cut into thin wedges
- 4 cloves garlic, chopped
- 1 stem lemongrass (white part only), finely chopped
- 2 bay leaves
- 1 large carrot, cut into 1 cm (½ inch) pieces on the diagonal
- 400 ml (13½ fl oz) can coconut milk

1 Remove the skin and any excess fat from the chicken. Pat dry with paper towels and cut each piece into 3 even pieces, making 12 pieces. Place the curry powder, sugar, ½ teaspoon black pepper and 2 teaspoons salt in a bowl, and mix well. Rub the curry mixture into the chicken pieces. Place the chicken on a plate, cover with plastic wrap and refrigerate overnight.

2 Heat the oil in a large saucepan. Add the sweet potato (yam) cubes and cook over medium heat for 3 minutes, or until lightly golden. Remove with a slotted spoon.

3 Remove all but 2 tablespoons of the oil from the pan. Add the onion and cook, stirring, for 5 minutes. Then add the garlic, lemongrass and bay leaves, and cook for 2 minutes.

4 Add the chicken and cook, stirring, over medium heat for 5 minutes, or until the chicken is well coated in the mixture and starting to change colour. Add 1 cup (250 ml / 8½ fl oz) water and simmer, covered, for 20 minutes. Stir once or twice.

5 Stir in the carrot, sweet potato (yam) and coconut milk, and simmer, uncovered, stirring occasionally, for 30 minutes, or until the chicken is cooked and tender. Be careful not to break up the sweet potato (yam) cubes. Serve with steamed rice or rice stick noodles.

FISH KOFTAS IN TOMATO CURRY

Preparation time:
40 minutes

Total cooking time:
30 minutes

Serves 6

INGREDIENTS

- 750 g (1 lb 10 oz) firm fish fillets, such as snapper or ling, roughly chopped
- 1 onion, chopped
- 2–3 cloves garlic, chopped
- 1 tablespoon grated fresh ginger (gingerroot)
- ⅓ cup (20 g/⅔ oz) chopped fresh coriander (cilantro) leaves
- 1 teaspoon garam masala
- ¼ teaspoon chilli powder
- 1 egg, lightly beaten
- oil, for shallow-frying

TOMATO CURRY SAUCE
- 2 tablespoons oil
- 1 large onion, finely chopped
- 3–4 cloves garlic, finely chopped
- 1 tablespoon grated fresh ginger (gingerroot)
- 1 teaspoon ground turmeric
- 1 teaspoon ground cumin
- 1 teaspoon ground coriander
- ½ teaspoon garam masala
- ¼ teaspoon chilli powder
- 2 × 400 g (14 oz) cans crushed tomatoes
- ¼ cup (25 g/¾ oz) chopped fresh coriander (cilantro)

1 Place the fish in a food processor and process until smooth. Add the onion, garlic, ginger (gingerroot), coriander (cilantro) leaves, garam masala, chilli powder and egg, and process using the pulse button until well combined. Using wetted hands, form 1 tablespoon of the mixture into a ball. Repeat with the remaining mixture.

2 To make the tomato curry sauce, heat the oil in a large saucepan, add the onion, garlic and ginger (gingerroot), and cook, stirring frequently, over medium heat for 8 minutes, or until lightly golden.

3 Add the spices and cook, stirring, for 2 minutes, or until aromatic. Add the crushed tomato and 1 cup (250 ml/ 8½ fl oz) water, then reduce the heat and simmer, stirring frequently, for 15 minutes, or until the sauce has reduced and thickened.

4 Meanwhile, heat 2 cm (¾ inch) of the oil in a large frying pan. Add the fish koftas in three to four batches and cook for 3 minutes, or until browned all over. Drain on paper towels.

5 Add the koftas to the sauce and simmer over low heat for 5 minutes, or until heated through. Gently fold in the coriander (cilantro), season with salt and serve with steamed rice and chapatis.

NOTE: The fish mixture is quite moist. Wetting your hands will stop the mixture from sticking to them.

BALINESE SEAFOOD CURRY

Preparation time:
20 minutes +
20 minutes marinating

Total cooking time:
20 minutes

Serves 6

INGREDIENTS

CURRY PASTE
- 2 tomatoes, peeled, seeded and roughly chopped
- 5 small fresh red chillies, seeded and chopped
- 5 cloves garlic, chopped
- 2 stems lemongrass (white part only), sliced
- 1 tablespoon coriander seeds, dry-roasted and ground
- 1 teaspoon shrimp powder, dry-roasted (see NOTE)
- 1 tablespoon ground almonds
- ¼ teaspoon ground nutmeg
- 1 teaspoon ground turmeric
- 3 tablespoons tamarind puree

- 1 tablespoon lime juice
- 250 g (8¾ oz) swordfish, cut into 3 cm (1¼ inch) cubes
- ¼ cup (60 ml/2 fl oz) oil
- 2 red onions, chopped
- 2 small fresh red chillies, seeded and sliced
- 400 g (14 oz) raw medium prawns (shrimp), peeled and deveined, tails intact
- 250 g (8¾ oz) calamari tubes, cut into 1 cm (½ inch) rings
- ½ cup (125 ml/4¼ fl oz) fish stock (broth)
- fresh Thai basil leaves, shredded, to garnish

1 To make the curry paste, place all the ingredients in a blender or food processor, and blend to a thick paste.

2 Place the lime juice in a bowl and season with salt and freshly ground black pepper. Add the swordfish, toss to coat well and leave to marinate for 20 minutes.

3 Heat the oil in a saucepan or wok, add the onion, sliced red chilli and curry paste, and cook, stirring occasionally, over low heat for 10 minutes, or until fragrant.

4 Add the swordfish and prawns (shrimp), and stir to coat in the curry paste mixture. Cook for 3 minutes, or until the prawns just turn pink, then add the calamari and cook for 1 minute.

5 Add the stock (broth) and bring to the boil, then reduce the heat and simmer for 2 minutes, or until the seafood is cooked and tender. Season to taste with salt and freshly ground black pepper. Garnish with the shredded fresh basil leaves.

NOTE: If you cannot purchase shrimp powder, place some dried baby shrimp in a mortar and pestle and grind to a fine powder. Alternatively, you can place them in the small bowl of a food processor and process to a fine powder.

PORK AND TAMARIND CURRY

Preparation time:
20 minutes

Total cooking time:
1 hour 50 minutes

Serves 6

INGREDIENTS

- ⅓ cup (80 ml/2¾ fl oz) oil
- 2 onions, thickly sliced
- 4 large cloves garlic, crushed
- 3 tablespoons Sri Lankan curry powder
- 1 tablespoon grated fresh ginger (gingerroot)
- 10 dried curry leaves or 5 fresh curry leaves
- 2 teaspoons chilli powder
- ¼ teaspoon fenugreek seeds
- 1.25 kg (2 lb 12 oz) lean shoulder pork, cubed

- 1 stem lemongrass (white part only), finely chopped
- 2 tablespoons tamarind puree
- 4 cardamom pods, crushed
- 400 ml (13½ fl oz) can coconut cream

CUCUMBER SAMBAL
- 1–2 large cucumbers, halved, seeded and finely chopped
- 2 cups (500 g/1 lb 2 oz) plain yoghurt
- 2 tablespoons fresh coriander (cilantro) leaves, finely chopped
- 1 tablespoon lemon juice
- 2 cloves garlic, crushed

1 Heat the oil in a heavy-based Dutch oven or deep, lidded frying pan. Add the onion, garlic, curry powder, ginger (gingerroot), curry leaves, chilli powder, fenugreek and 1 teaspoon salt, and cook, stirring, over medium heat for 5 minutes.

2 Add the pork, lemongrass, tamarind puree, cardamom and 1½ cups (375 ml/13 fl oz) hot water, then reduce the heat and simmer, covered, for 1 hour.

3 Stir in the coconut cream and simmer, uncovered, for 40–45 minutes, or until the sauce has reduced and become thick and creamy.

4 To make the cucumber sambal, place the cucumber in a bowl and stir in the yoghurt, coriander (cilantro), lemon juice and garlic. Season to taste.

5 Serve the curry with the cucumber sambal and steamed basmati rice.

SPICY SEAFOOD CURRY

Preparation time:
30 minutes + 15 minutes standing

Total cooking time:
1 hour

Serves 4–6

INGREDIENTS

- 1 kg (2 lb 3 oz) raw medium prawns (shrimp), peeled and deveined, tails intact (reserve shells and heads)
- 1 teaspoon ground turmeric
- ¼ cup (60 ml/2 fl oz) oil
- 2 onions, finely chopped
- 4–6 cloves garlic, finely chopped
- 1–2 small fresh green chillies, seeded and chopped
- 2 teaspoons ground cumin
- 2 teaspoons ground coriander
- 1 teaspoon paprika
- ⅓ cup (90 g/3¼ oz) plain yoghurt
- ⅓ cup (80 ml/2¾ fl oz) thick cream
- ⅓ cup (20 g/¾ oz) chopped fresh coriander (cilantro) leaves

1 Bring 1 litre (1.1 US qt/ 1.75 UK qt) water to the boil in a large saucepan. Add the reserved prawn (shrimp) shells and heads, reduce the heat and simmer for 2 minutes. Skim any scum that forms on the surface during cooking with a skimmer or slotted spoon. Drain, discard the shells and heads, and return the liquid to the pan. You will need 3 cups (750 ml/26 fl oz) liquid. Make up with water, if necessary. Add the turmeric and peeled prawns (shrimp), and cook for 1 minute, or until the prawns just turn pink. Remove the prawns and set the stock (broth) aside.

2 Heat the oil in a large saucepan. Cook the onion, stirring, for 8 minutes, or until light golden brown. Take care not to burn the onion. Add the garlic and chilli, cook for 2 minutes, then add the cumin, coriander and paprika, and cook, stirring, for 2–3 minutes, or until fragrant.

3 Gradually add the reserved prawn stock (shrimp broth), bring to the boil and cook, stirring occasionally, for 35 minutes, or until the mixture has reduced by half and thickened.

4 Remove from the heat and stir in the yoghurt. Add the prawns (shrimp) and stir over low heat for 2–3 minutes, or until the prawns are warmed through, but do now allow the mixture to boil. Stir in the cream and coriander (cilantro) leaves. Cover and leave to stand for 15 minutes to allow the flavours to infuse. Reheat gently and serve with rice.

NOTE: You can remove the prawn tails, if you prefer.

CHUNKY VEGETABLE SOUP

Preparation time:
20 minutes + overnight
soaking

Total cooking time:
1 hour 5 minutes

Serves 6

INGREDIENTS

- ½ cup (100 g/3½ oz) dried red kidney beans or borlotti (romano) beans
- 1 tablespoon olive oil
- 1 leek, halved lengthways, chopped
- 1 small onion, diced
- 2 carrots, chopped
- 2 celery sticks (ribs), chopped
- 1 large zucchini (courgette), chopped
- 1 tablespoon tomato paste (tomato puree)

- 1 litre (1.1 US qt/1.75 UK qt) vegetable stock (broth)
- 400 g (14 oz) pumpkin, cut into 2 cm (¾ inch) cubes
- 2 potatoes, cut into 2 cm (¾ inch) cubes
- ¼ cup (7 g/¼ oz) chopped fresh flat-leaf parsley

1 Put the beans in a large bowl, cover with cold water and soak overnight. Rinse, then transfer to a saucepan, cover with cold water and cook for 45 minutes, or until just tender. Drain.

2 Meanwhile, heat the oil in a large saucepan. Add the leek and onion, and cook over medium heat for 2–3 minutes without browning, or until they start to soften. Add the carrot, celery and zucchini (courgette), and cook for 3–4 minutes. Add the tomato paste (tomato puree) and stir for a further 1 minute. Pour in the stock (broth) and 1.25 litres (1.3 US qt/1.1 UK qt) water, and bring to the boil. Reduce the heat to low and simmer for 20 minutes.

3 Add the pumpkin, potato, parsley and beans, and simmer for a further 20 minutes, or until the vegetables are tender and the beans are cooked. Season to taste. Serve immediately with crusty wholemeal or wholegrain bread.

NOTE: To save time, use a 420 g (14¾ oz) can of red kidney beans instead of dried beans.

AUTUMN VEGETABLE STEW

Preparation time:
25 minutes

Total cooking time:
30 minutes

Serves 4–6

INGREDIENTS

- 185 g (6½ oz) frozen broad (fava) beans, thawed
- 150 g (5¼ oz) baby onions
- 50 g (1¾ oz) butter
- 2 teaspoons olive oil
- 400 g (14 oz) small parsnips
- 150 g (5¼ oz) Jerusalem artichokes
- 2 tablespoons plain (all-purpose) flour
- 2⅓ cups (580 ml/19¾ fl oz) vegetable stock (broth)
- 300 ml (10 fl oz) cream
- 2 teaspoons grated lemon rind
- 1 teaspoon grated orange rind
- 400 g (14 oz) baby carrots, trimmed
- 500 g (1 lb 2 oz) baby turnips, trimmed

1 Peel and discard the tough outer skin of the broad (fava) beans. Carefully peel the onions, leaving the flat root end attached, then cut a cross through the root end of each onion.

2 Heat the butter and oil in a large, heavy-based saucepan until foamy. Add the onions and cook for 7 minutes over low–medium heat, turning often to colour evenly.

3 While the onions are browning, peel the parsnips and artichokes, and cut them into bite-size pieces. Add to the saucepan and toss well. Scatter the flour over the onion, parsnip and artichokes, toss to coat and cook for 2 minutes.

4 Stir in the chicken stock (broth), cream, lemon rind and orange rind. Bring to the boil, stirring, then reduce the heat and simmer for 7 minutes, or until the vegetables are half-cooked.

5 Add the carrots and turnips, and toss well. Cover the pan and cook for 4–5 minutes, or until the vegetables are just tender. Season well with salt and freshly ground pepper, stir in the peeled broad (fava) beans to heat through, and serve.

NOTES: Baby vegetables have a sweet, delicate flavour. If unavailable, choose the smallest vegetables and cook them for a few minutes longer.

Fresh broad (fava) beans can be used. Add them with the carrots and turnips.

SPICY VEGETABLE STEW WITH DHAL

Preparation time:	**Total cooking time:**	**Serves** 4–6
25 minutes + 2 hours soaking	1 hour 35 minutes	

INGREDIENTS

DHAL
- ¾ cup (165 g/5¾ oz) yellow split peas
- 5 cm (2 inch) piece fresh ginger (gingerroot), grated
- 2–3 cloves garlic, crushed
- 1 fresh red chilli, seeded and chopped

- 2 tablespoons oil
- 1 teaspoon yellow mustard seeds
- 1 teaspoon cumin seeds
- 1 teaspoon ground cumin
- ½ teaspoon garam masala
- 1 red onion, cut into thin wedges

- 3 tomatoes, peeled, seeded and chopped
- 3 slender eggplants (aubergines), cut into 2 cm (¾ inch) slices
- 2 carrots, cut into 2 cm (¾ inch) slices
- ¼ cauliflower, cut into florets
- 1½ cups (375 ml/13 fl oz) vegetable stock (broth)
- 2 small zucchini (courgettes), cut into 3 cm (1¼ inch) slices
- ½ cup (80 g/2¾ oz) frozen peas
- ½ cup (15 g/½ oz) fresh coriander (cilantro) leaves

1 To make the dhal, place the split peas in a bowl, cover with water and soak for 2 hours. Drain. Place in a large saucepan with the ginger (gingerroot), garlic, chilli and 3 cups (750 ml/26 fl oz) water. Bring to the boil, then reduce the heat and simmer for 45 minutes, or until soft.

2 Heat the oil in a large saucepan. Cook the spices over medium heat for 30 seconds, or until fragrant. Add the onion and cook for a further 2 minutes, or until the onion is soft. Stir in the tomato, eggplant (aubergine), carrot and cauliflower.

3 Add the dhal puree and stock
(broth), mix together well and
simmer, covered, for 45 minutes,
or until the vegetables are tender.
Stir occasionally. Add the zucchini
(courgette) and peas during the
last 10 minutes of cooking. Stir in
the coriander (cilantro) leaves and
serve hot.

LENTIL BHUJIA STEW

Preparation time:
30 minutes + overnight soaking +
30 minutes refrigeration

Total cooking time:
1 hour 10 minutes

Serves 4–6

INGREDIENTS

- 2 cups (370 g / 13 oz) green or brown lentils
- 1 large onion, grated
- 1 large potato, grated
- 1 teaspoon ground cumin
- 1 teaspoon ground coriander
- 1 teaspoon ground turmeric
- ¾ cup (90 g / 3¼ oz) plain (all-purpose) flour
- oil, for shallow-frying
- 2 cloves garlic, crushed
- 1 tablespoon grated fresh ginger (gingerroot)
- 1 cup (250 ml / 8½ fl oz) pureed tomato
- 2 cups (500 ml / 17 fl oz) vegetable stock (broth)
- 1 cup (250 ml / 8½ fl oz) cream
- 200 g (7 oz) green beans, topped, tailed and cut in half
- 2 carrots, sliced
- 2 hard-boiled eggs, chopped
- sprigs fresh rosemary, to garnish

1 Soak the lentils overnight in cold water. Drain well. Squeeze the excess moisture from the lentils, onion and potato using a tea towel. Place them in a bowl with the ground spices and flour; mix well and leave for 10 minutes. With floured hands, shape the mixture into walnut-sized balls and place on a foil-lined tray (sheet). Cover and refrigerate for 30 minutes.

2 Heat 2 cm (¾ inch) of oil in a heavy-based frying pan. Cook the balls in batches over high heat until golden brown. Drain on paper towels.

3 Heat 2 tablespoons of oil in a saucepan and gently fry the garlic and ginger (gingerroot) for 2 minutes. Stir in the puree, stock (broth) and cream. Bring to the boil, then reduce the heat and simmer for 10 minutes. Add the beans, lentil balls and carrot. Cook, covered, for 30 minutes, stirring twice. Add the egg and cook for 10 minutes. Garnish with rosemary to serve.

VARIATION: Split peas can be used in this recipe in place of the lentils. Soak them in cold water overnight, then drain well before using.

PASTA AND BEAN SOUP

Preparation time:
15 minutes + overnight soaking +
10 minutes resting

Total cooking time:
1 hour 45 minutes

Serves 4

INGREDIENTS

- 200 g (7 oz) dried borlotti
  (romano) beans
- ¼ cup (60 ml/2 fl oz) olive oil
- 1 onion, finely chopped
- 2 cloves garlic, crushed
- 1 celery stick (rib), thinly sliced
- 1 carrot, diced
- 1 bay leaf
- 1 sprig fresh rosemary
- 1 sprig fresh flat-leaf parsley
- 400 g (14 oz) can diced
  tomatoes, drained
- 1.6 litres (1.7 US qt/1.4 UK qt)
  vegetable stock (broth)
- 2 tablespoons finely chopped fresh
  flat-leaf parsley
- 150 g (5¼ oz) ditalini or other small
  dried pasta
- extra virgin olive oil, to serve
- grated fresh Parmesan, to serve

1 Place the beans in a large bowl,
cover with cold water and leave to
soak overnight. Drain and rinse.

2 Heat the oil in a large saucepan,
add the onion, garlic, celery and
carrot, and cook over medium
heat for 5 minutes, or until
golden. Season with pepper. Add
the bay leaf, rosemary, parsley,
tomato, stock (broth) and beans,
and bring to the boil. Reduce the
heat and simmer for 1½ hours, or
until the beans are tender. Add
more boiling water if necessary
to maintain the liquid level.

3 Discard the bay leaf, rosemary
and parsley sprigs. Scoop out
1 cup (250 ml/8½ fl oz) of the
bean mixture and puree in a food
processor or blender. Return to
the pan, season with salt and
ground black pepper, and add the
parsley and pasta. Simmer for
6 minutes, or until the pasta is al
dente. Remove from the heat and
set aside for 10 minutes. Serve
drizzled with extra virgin olive
oil and sprinkled with Parmesan.

NOTE: If you prefer, you can use
three 400 g (14 oz) cans drained
borlotti (romano) beans. Simmer
with the other vegetables for
30 minutes.

SPICED LENTIL SOUP

Preparation time:
10 minutes + 20 minutes standing

Total cooking time:
50 minutes

Serves 4

INGREDIENTS

- 1 eggplant (aubergine)
- ¼ cup (60 ml/2 fl oz) olive oil
- 1 onion, finely chopped
- 2 teaspoons brown mustard seeds
- 2 teaspoons ground cumin
- 1 teaspoon garam masala
- ¼ teaspoon cayenne (red) pepper (optional)
- 2 large carrots, cut into cubes
- 1 celery stick (rib), diced
- 400 g (14 oz) can crushed tomatoes
- 1 cup (110 g/3¾ oz) Puy lentils
- 1 litre (1.1 US qt/1.75 UK pt) vegetable stock (broth)
- ¾ cup (35 g/1¼ oz) roughly chopped fresh coriander (cilantro) leaves
- ½ cup (125 g/4⅓ oz) plain yoghurt

1 Cut the eggplant (aubergine) into cubes, place in a colander, sprinkle with salt and leave for 20 minutes. Rinse well and pat dry with paper towels.

2 Heat the oil in a large saucepan over medium heat. Add the onion and cook for 5 minutes, or until softened. Add the eggplant (aubergine), stir to coat in oil and cook for 3 minutes, or until softened.

3 Add all the spices and cook, stirring, for 1 minute, or until fragrant and the mustard seeds begin to pop. Add the carrot and celery and cook for 1 minute. Stir in the tomato, lentils and stock (broth) and bring to the boil. Reduce the heat and simmer for 40 minutes, or until the lentils are tender and the liquid is reduced to a thick stew-like soup. Season to taste with salt and cracked black pepper.

4 Stir the coriander (cilantro) into the soup just before serving. Ladle the soup into four warmed bowls and serve with a dollop of the yoghurt on top.

MEXICAN BEAN CHOWDER

Preparation time:
20 minutes + overnight
soaking

Total cooking time:
1 hour 15 minutes

Serves 6

INGREDIENTS

- ¾ cup (155 g/5½ oz) dried red kidney beans
- ¾ cup (165 g/5¾ oz) dried Mexican black beans (see NOTE)
- 1 tablespoon oil
- 1 onion, chopped
- 2 cloves garlic, crushed
- ½–1 teaspoon chilli powder
- 1 tablespoon ground cumin
- 2 teaspoons ground coriander
- 2 × 400 g (14 oz) cans chopped tomatoes

- 3 cups (750 ml/26 fl oz) vegetable stock (broth)
- 1 red capsicum (pepper), chopped
- 1 green capsicum (pepper), chopped
- 440 g (15½ oz) can corn kernels
- 2 tablespoons tomato paste (tomato puree)
- grated Cheddar (American) cheese, to serve
- sour cream, to serve

1 Soak the kidney beans and black beans in separate bowls in plenty of cold water overnight. Drain. Place in a large saucepan, cover with water and bring to the boil. Reduce the heat and simmer for 45 minutes, or until tender. Drain.

2 Heat the oil in a large saucepan, add the onion and cook over medium heat until soft. Add the garlic, chilli powder, cumin and coriander, and cook for 1 minute. Stir in the tomato, stock (broth), capsicum (pepper), corn and tomato paste (tomato puree). Cook, covered, for 25–30 minutes. Add the beans during the last 10 minutes of cooking. Stir occasionally.

3 Serve topped with the grated Cheddar (American) cheese and a spoonful of sour cream.

NOTE: Mexican black beans are also known as black turtle beans.

MATTAR PANEER

Preparation time:
30 minutes +
30 minutes draining +
4 hours setting

Total cooking time:
40 minutes

Serves 6

INGREDIENTS

PANEER
• 2 litres (2.1 US qt/1.75 UK qt)
  full-cream milk
• ⅓ cup (80 ml/2¾ fl oz) lemon juice
• oil, for deep-frying

CURRY PASTE
• 2 large onions
• 3 cloves garlic
• 1 teaspoon grated fresh
  ginger (gingerroot)
• 1 teaspoon cumin seeds
• 3 dried red chillies

• 1 teaspoon cardamom seeds
• 4 cloves
• 1 teaspoon fennel seeds
• 2 pieces cassia bark
• 500 g (1 lb 2 oz) frozen peas
• 2 tablespoons oil
• 400 g (14 oz) pureed tomato
• 1 tablespoon garam masala
• 1 teaspoon ground coriander
• ¼ teaspoon ground turmeric
• 1 tablespoon cream
• fresh coriander (cilantro) leaves,
  to garnish

1 Place the milk in a large
saucepan, bring to the boil, stir
in the lemon juice and turn off
the heat. Stir the mixture for
1–2 seconds as it curdles. Place
in a colander and leave for
30 minutes for the whey to
drain off. Place the paneer curds

on a clean, flat surface, cover
with a plate, weigh down and
leave for at least 4 hours.

2 To make the curry paste, place the
ingredients in a spice grinder or
mortar and pestle, and grind to a
smooth paste.

3 Cut the solid paneer into 2 cm (¾ inch) cubes. Fill a deep heavy-based saucepan one-third full of oil and heat to 180°C (350°F), or until a cube of bread browns in 15 seconds. Cook the paneer in batches for 2–3 minutes, or until golden. Drain on paper towels.

4 Cook the peas in a saucepan of boiling water for 3 minutes, or until tender. Drain.

5 Heat the oil in a large saucepan, add the curry paste and cook over medium heat for 4 minutes, or until fragrant. Add the pureed tomato, spices, cream and ½ cup (125 ml/4¼ fl oz) water. Season with salt, and simmer over medium heat for 5 minutes. Add the paneer and peas, and cook for 3 minutes. Garnish with fresh coriander (cilantro) leaves, and serve hot.

VEGETABLE CURRY

Preparation time:
20 minutes

Total cooking time:
30 minutes

Serves 6

INGREDIENTS

- 250 g (8¾ oz) potatoes, cut into
  2 cm (¾ inch) cubes
- 250 g (8¾ oz) pumpkin, cut into
  2 cm (¾ inch) cubes
- 200 g (7 oz) cauliflower, broken
  into florets
- 150 g (5¼ oz) yellow squash,
  quartered
- 2 tablespoons oil
- 2 onions, chopped
- 3 tablespoons Indian curry powder
- 400 g (14 oz) can crushed tomatoes
- 1 cup (250 ml/8½ fl oz) vegetable
  stock (broth)
- 150 g (5¼ oz) green beans, cut into
  4 cm (1½ inch) lengths
- ⅓ cup (90 g/3¼ oz) plain yoghurt
- ¼ cup (40 g/1½ oz) sultanas
  (golden raisins)

1 Cook the potato and pumpkin in
  a saucepan of boiling water for
  6 minutes, then remove. Add the
  cauliflower and yellow squash,
  cook for 4 minutes, then remove.

2 Heat the oil in a large saucepan,
  add the onion and cook, stirring,
  over medium heat for 8 minutes,
  or until starting to brown.

3 Add the Indian curry powder and
  stir for 1 minute, or until
  fragrant. Stir in the crushed
  tomato and vegetable stock
  (broth), and combine well.

4 Add the chopped potato,
  pumpkin, cauliflower and yellow
  squash, and cook for 5 minutes,
  then add the green beans and
  cook for a further 2–3 minutes,
  or until the vegetables are
  just tender.

5 Add the yoghurt and sultanas
  (golden raisins), and stir to
  combine. Simmer for 3 minutes,
  or until thickened slightly.
  Season to taste with salt and
  black pepper, and serve with
  lemon wedges.

CHANNA MASALA

Preparation time:
10 minutes + overnight soaking

Total cooking time:
1 hour 15 minutes

Serves 6

INGREDIENTS

- 1 cup (220 g/7¾ oz) dried chickpeas (garbanzo beans)
- 2 tablespoons oil
- 2 onions, finely chopped
- 2 large ripe tomatoes, chopped
- ½ teaspoon ground coriander
- 1 teaspoon ground cumin
- 1 teaspoon chilli powder
- ¼ teaspoon ground turmeric
- 1 tablespoon channa (chole) masala (see NOTE)
- 20 g (⅔ oz) ghee or butter
- 1 small white onion, sliced
- fresh mint and coriander (cilantro) leaves, to garnish

1 Place the chickpeas (garbanzo beans) in a bowl, cover with water and leave to soak overnight. Drain, rinse and place in a large saucepan. Cover with plenty of water and bring to the boil, then reduce the heat and simmer for 40 minutes, or until soft. Drain.

2 Heat the oil in a large saucepan, add the onion and cook over medium heat for 15 minutes, or until golden brown. Add the tomato, ground coriander and cumin, chilli powder, turmeric, channa (chole) masala and 2 cups (500 ml/17 fl oz) cold water, and cook for 10 minutes, or until the tomato is soft. Add the chickpeas (garbanzo beans), season well with salt and cook for 7–10 minutes, or until the sauce thickens. Transfer to a serving dish. Place the ghee or butter on top and allow to melt before serving. Garnish with sliced onion and fresh mint and coriander (cilantro) leaves.

NOTE: Channa (chole) masala is a spice blend specifically used in this dish. It is available at Indian grocery stores. Garam masala can be used as a substitute, but this will alter the final flavour.

DUM ALU

Preparation time:
20 minutes

Total cooking time:
30 minutes

Serves 6

INGREDIENTS

CURRY PASTE
- 4 cardamom pods
- 1 teaspoon grated fresh
  ginger (gingerroot)
- 2 cloves garlic
- 6 small fresh red chillies
- 1 teaspoon cumin seeds
- ¼ cup (40 g/1½ oz) raw cashew
  nut pieces
- 1 tablespoon white poppy seeds
  (khus) (see NOTE)
- 1 cinnamon stick
- 6 cloves

- 1 kg (2 lb 3 oz) potatoes, cubed
- 2 onions, roughly chopped
- 2 tablespoons oil
- ½ teaspoon ground turmeric
- 1 teaspoon besan (chickpea/
  garbanzo bean flour)
- 1 cup (250 g/8¾ oz) plain yoghurt
- fresh coriander (cilantro) leaves,
  to garnish

1 To make the curry paste, lightly
  crush the cardamom pods with
  the flat side of a heavy knife.
  Remove the seeds, discarding the
  pods. Place the seeds and the
  remaining curry paste ingredients
  in a food processor, and process
  to a smooth paste.

2 Bring a large saucepan of lightly
  salted water to the boil. Add the
  potato and cook for 5–6 minutes,
  or until just tender. Drain.

3 Place the onion in a food
  processor and process in short
  bursts until it is finely ground
  but not pureed. Heat the oil in a
  large saucepan, add the ground
  onion and cook over low heat
  for 5 minutes. Add the curry
  paste and cook, stirring, for a
  further 5 minutes, or until
  fragrant. Stir in the potato,
  turmeric, salt to taste and 1 cup
  (250 ml/8½ fl oz) water.

4 Reduce the heat and simmer,
  tightly covered, for 10 minutes,
  or until the potato is cooked but
  not breaking up and the sauce has
  thickened slightly.

5 Combine the besan (chickpea/
garbanzo bean flour) with the
yoghurt, add to the potato
mixture and cook, stirring,
over low heat for 5 minutes,
or until thickened again.
Garnish with the coriander
(cilantro) leaves.

NOTE: White poppy seeds (khus)
should not be mistaken for black
and do not yield opium. They are
off-white, odourless and flavourless
until roasted when they have a
slight sesame aroma and flavour. If
they are not available, replace the
poppy seeds with sesame seeds.

MUSAMAN VEGETABLE CURRY

Preparation time:
25 minutes

Total cooking time:
45 minutes

Serves 4–6

INGREDIENTS

CURRY PASTE
- 1 tablespoon oil
- 1 teaspoon coriander seeds
- 1 teaspoon cumin seeds
- 8 cloves
- ½ teaspoon fennel seeds
- seeds from 4 cardamom pods
- 6 red Asian shallots, chopped
- 3 cloves garlic, chopped
- 1 teaspoon finely chopped lemongrass (white part only)
- 1 teaspoon finely chopped fresh galangal
- 4 large dried red chillies
- 1 teaspoon ground nutmeg
- 1 teaspoon white pepper
- 1 tablespoon oil
- 250 g (8¾ oz) baby onions

- 500 g (1 lb 2 oz) small new potatoes
- 300 g (10½ oz) carrots, cut into 3 cm (1¼ inch) pieces
- 225 g (8 oz) can whole champignons, drained
- 1 cinnamon stick
- 1 kaffir lime leaf
- 1 bay leaf
- 1 cup (250 ml/8½ fl oz) coconut cream
- 1 tablespoon lime juice
- 3 teaspoons grated palm sugar or soft brown sugar
- 1 tablespoon shredded fresh Thai basil leaves
- 1 tablespoon crushed roasted peanuts
- fresh Thai basil leaves, extra, to garnish

1 To make the curry paste, heat the oil in a frying pan over low heat, add the coriander, cumin, cloves, fennel seeds and cardamom seeds, and cook for 1–2 minutes, or until fragrant.

Place in a food processor and add the shallots, garlic, lemongrass, galangal, chillies, nutmeg and white pepper. Process until smooth, adding a little water as necessary.

2 Heat the oil in a large saucepan, add the curry paste and cook, stirring, over medium heat for 2 minutes, or until fragrant. Add the vegetables, cinnamon stick, kaffir lime leaf and bay leaf, and season with salt. Add enough water to cover – about 2 cups (500 ml / 17 fl oz) – and bring to the boil. Reduce the heat and simmer, covered, stirring frequently, for 30–35 minutes, or until the vegetables are cooked. Stir in the coconut cream and cook, uncovered, for 4 minutes, stirring frequently, until thickened slightly. Stir in the lime juice, palm sugar or brown sugar and shredded Thai basil. Add a little water if the sauce is too dry. Garnish with the peanuts and Thai basil leaves.

YELLOW VEGETABLE CURRY

Preparation time:
20 minutes

Total cooking time:
45 minutes

Serves 6

INGREDIENTS

- ¼ cup (60 ml/2 fl oz) oil
- 1 onion, finely chopped
- 2 tablespoons yellow curry paste
- 250 g (8¾ oz) potato, diced
- 200 g (7 oz) zucchini (courgette), diced
- 150 g (5¼ oz) red capsicum (pepper), diced
- 100 g (3½ oz) beans, trimmed
- 50 g (1¾ oz) bamboo shoots, sliced
- 1 cup (250 ml/8½ fl oz) vegetable stock (broth)
- 400 ml (13½ fl oz) can coconut cream
- fresh Thai basil leaves, to garnish

1 Heat the oil in a large saucepan, add the onion and cook over medium heat for 4–5 minutes, or until softened and just turning golden. Add the yellow curry paste and cook, stirring, for 2 minutes, or until fragrant.

2 Add all the vegetables and cook, stirring, over high heat for 2 minutes. Pour in the vegetable stock (broth), reduce the heat to medium and cook, covered, for 15–20 minutes, or until the vegetables are tender. Cook, uncovered, over high heat for 5–10 minutes, or until the sauce has reduced slightly.

3 Stir in the coconut cream, and season with salt. Bring to the boil, stirring frequently, then reduce the heat and simmer for 5 minutes. Garnish with the Thai basil leaves.

VEGETABLE TAGINE

Preparation time:
20 minutes

Total cooking time:
1 hour

Serves 4–6

INGREDIENTS

- 2 tablespoons oil
- 2 onions, chopped
- 1 teaspoon ground ginger
- 2 teaspoons ground paprika
- 2 teaspoons ground cumin
- 1 cinnamon stick
- pinch saffron threads
- 1.5 kg (3 lb 5 oz) vegetables, peeled and cut into large chunks (carrot, eggplant (aubergine), orange sweet potato (yam), parsnip, potato, pumpkin)
- ½ preserved lemon, rinsed, pith and flesh removed, thinly sliced

- 400 g (14 oz) can peeled tomatoes
- 1 cup (250 ml/8½ fl oz) vegetable stock (broth)
- 100 g (3½ oz) dried pears, halved
- 50 g (1¾ oz) pitted prunes (dried plums)
- 2 zucchini (courgettes), cut into large chunks
- 300 g (10½ oz) couscous
- 1 tablespoon olive oil
- ¼ cup (7 g/¼ oz) chopped fresh flat-leaf parsley
- ⅓ cup (50 g/1¾ oz) almonds

1 Preheat the oven to moderate 180°C (350°F/Gas 4). Heat the oil in a large saucepan or ovenproof dish, add the onion and cook over medium heat for 5 minutes, or until soft. Add the spices and cook for 3 minutes.

2 Add the vegetables and cook, stirring, until coated with the spices and the vegetables begin to soften. Add the lemon, tomatoes,

stock (broth), pears and prunes (dried plums). Cover, transfer to the oven and cook for 30 minutes. Add the zucchini (courgette) and cook for 15–20 minutes, or until the vegetables are tender.

3 Cover the couscous with the olive oil and 2 cups (500 ml/17 fl oz) boiling water, and stand until all the water has been absorbed. Fluff with a fork.

4 Remove the cinnamon stick from the vegetables, then stir in the parsley. Serve on a large platter with the couscous formed into a ring and the vegetable tagine in the centre, sprinkled with the almonds.

VEGETARIAN CHILLI

Preparation time:
15 minutes +
10 minutes soaking

Total cooking time:
40 minutes

Serves 6–8

INGREDIENTS

- ¾ cup (130 g/4½ oz) burghul
- 2 tablespoons olive oil
- 1 large onion, finely chopped
- 2 cloves garlic, crushed
- 1 teaspoon chilli powder
- 2 teaspoons ground cumin
- 1 teaspoon cayenne (red) pepper
- ½ teaspoon ground cinnamon
- 2 × 400 g (14 oz) cans
  crushed tomatoes

- 3 cups (750 ml/26 fl oz) vegetable
  stock (broth)
- 440 g (15½ oz) can red kidney beans,
  rinsed and drained
- 2 × 300 g (10½ oz) cans chickpeas
  (garbanzo beans), rinsed and drained
- 310 g (11 oz) can corn kernels, drained
- 2 tablespoons tomato paste
  (tomato puree)
- corn (nacho) chips and sour cream

1 Soak the burghul with 1 cup
(250 ml/8½ fl oz) hot water for
10 minutes. Heat the oil in a
large heavy-based saucepan and
cook the onion for 10 minutes,
stirring often, until soft and
golden.

2 Add the garlic, chilli powder,
cumin, cayenne (red) pepper and
cinnamon, and cook, stirring, for
1 minute.

3 Add the tomato, stock (broth)
and burghul. Bring to the boil
and simmer for 10 minutes. Stir
in the beans, drained chickpeas
(garbanzo beans), corn and
tomato paste (tomato puree), and
simmer for 20 minutes, stirring
often. Serve with corn (nacho)
chips and sour cream.

RATATOUILLE

Preparation time:
30 minutes
Total cooking time:
40 minutes
Serves 4–6

INGREDIENTS

- 100 ml (3½ fl oz) olive oil
- 500 g (1 lb 2 oz) eggplant (aubergine), cut into 2 cm (¾ inch) cubes
- 375 g (13¼ oz) zucchini (courgette), cut into 2 cm (¾ inch) slices
- 1 green capsicum (pepper), seeded, cut into 2 cm (¾ inch) cubes
- 1 red onion, cut into 2 cm (¾ inch) wedges
- 3 cloves garlic, finely chopped
- ¼ teaspoon cayenne (red) pepper
- 2 teaspoons chopped fresh thyme
- 2 bay leaves
- 6 vine-ripened tomatoes, peeled and roughly chopped
- 1 tablespoon red wine vinegar
- 1 teaspoon caster (berry) sugar
- ¼ cup (15 g/½ oz) shredded fresh basil

1 Heat 2 tablespoons of the oil in a large saucepan and cook the eggplant (aubergine) over medium heat for 4–5 minutes, or until soft but not browned. Remove all the eggplant (aubergine) from the pan.

2 Add 2 tablespoons oil to the pan and cook the zucchini (courgette) slices for 3–4 minutes, or until softened. Remove the zucchini (courgette) from the pan. Add the capsicum (pepper) to the pan, cook for 2 minutes, then remove.

3 Heat the remaining oil in the pan, add the onion wedges and cook for 2–3 minutes, or until softened. Add the garlic, cayenne (red) pepper, thyme and bay leaves, and cook, stirring, for 1 minute. Return the cooked eggplant (aubergine), zucchini (courgette) and capsicum (pepper) to the pan, and add the tomato, vinegar and sugar. Simmer for 20 minutes, stirring occasionally. Stir in the basil and season with salt and black pepper. Serve hot or cold.

NOTE: Ratatouille takes quite a long time to prepare and so is traditionally made in large quantities. It is then eaten over several days as an hors d'oeuvre, side dish or main meal.

CREAMY POTATO AND PARSNIP MASH

Preparation time:
10 minutes

Total cooking time:
20 minutes

Serves 4–6

INGREDIENTS

- 2 large potatoes
- 5 large parsnips
- 30 g (1 oz) butter
- 1 tablespoon milk
- 2 tablespoons sour cream
- chopped fresh chives, to garnish

1 Peel the potatoes and parsnips, then chop into even-sized pieces. Cook them in a large saucepan of lightly salted boiling water for about 20 minutes, or until soft.

2 Drain well, then transfer to a bowl and mash with the butter, milk and sour cream until smooth and fluffy. Season generously with salt and freshly ground pepper. Sprinkle with chives and serve at once.

NOTE: Sebago, bison, coliban, nicola, pontiac and King Edward are some good all-purpose potatoes that give successful results in this recipe.

PEA PUREE

Preparation time:
30 minutes

Total cooking time:
15 minutes

Serves 4

INGREDIENTS

- 30 g (1 oz) butter
- 1 large leek, finely chopped
- 1 tablespoon finely chopped
  fresh mint
- 1 chicken stock (bouillon)
  cube, crumbled
- 1 kg (2 lb 3 oz) fresh peas, shelled
- 1 large lettuce leaf, shredded
- 2 tablespoons sour cream
- 1 tablespoon chopped fresh chives
- 1–2 whole fresh chives, to garnish

1 Melt the butter in a saucepan and gently fry the leek for 5 minutes, or until softened but not browned.

2 Stir in the mint, stock (bouillon) cube, peas, lettuce and just enough water to cover the peas. Bring to the boil, then reduce the heat to low and simmer for 8–10 minutes, or until the peas are tender. Do not overcook or the peas will lose their bright colour.

3 Drain thoroughly, transfer to a food processor and blend until smooth. Season to taste with salt and white pepper, stir in the sour cream and chopped chives, and serve at once, garnished with whole chives.

NOTE: Instead of fresh peas, you could use 3 cups (450 g/15¾ oz) frozen peas. Reduce the cooking time to 3–4 minutes.

CAULIFLOWER AND FENNEL PUREE

Preparation time:
10 minutes

Total cooking time:
25 minutes

Serves 6

INGREDIENTS

- 1 medium fennel bulb (see NOTE)
- 1 large cauliflower, trimmed
- 90 g (3¼ oz) butter
- 1 tablespoon cider vinegar or white wine vinegar
- 1 teaspoon salt
- ¼ teaspoon sugar

1 Reserving the fronds, trim the fennel and finely chop the bulb and thin green stems. Set the stems aside. Cut the cauliflower into florets.

2 In a large saucepan, melt 60 g (2 oz) of the butter and gently fry the chopped fennel bulb for 5 minutes, stirring occasionally. Add the cauliflower, toss to coat and cook for 1–2 minutes, then add enough water to just cover.

3 Add the vinegar, salt and sugar, and bring to the boil. Reduce the heat and simmer for 15 minutes, or until the cauliflower is very tender. Drain thoroughly, then transfer to a food processor and blend to a smooth puree. Stir in the rest of the butter and the chopped fennel stems. Season to taste and garnish with fennel fronds.

NOTE: Fennel bulbs are usually sold already trimmed but, if possible, buy an untrimmed bulb for this recipe, so you can use the stalks to add flavour, and the fronds to garnish.

MASH WITH GINGER AND GARLIC

Preparation time:
15 minutes

Total cooking time:
20 minutes

Serves 4

INGREDIENTS

- 750 g (1 lb 10 oz) orange sweet potatoes (yams)
- 45 g (1⅔ oz) butter, chopped
- 1 clove garlic, crushed
- 2 teaspoons grated fresh ginger (gingerroot)
- 1½ tablespoons chopped fresh coriander (cilantro)
- 2 teaspoons soy sauce
- sprigs fresh coriander (cilantro), to garnish

1 Peel the sweet potatoes (yams) and cut them into even-sized pieces. Cook the sweet potato (yam) in a saucepan of lightly salted boiling water for 10–15 minutes, or until tender. Drain.

2 Melt the butter in a small pan and add the garlic and ginger (gingerroot). Cook over low heat, stirring, for 1 minute.

3 Mash the hot sweet potato (yam) until almost smooth. Stir through the garlic mixture, chopped coriander (cilantro) and soy sauce. Garnish with coriander (cilantro) sprigs and serve immediately.

NOTE: Orange sweet potato (yam) is sweeter than regular potatoes, with a texture between a potato and a pumpkin.

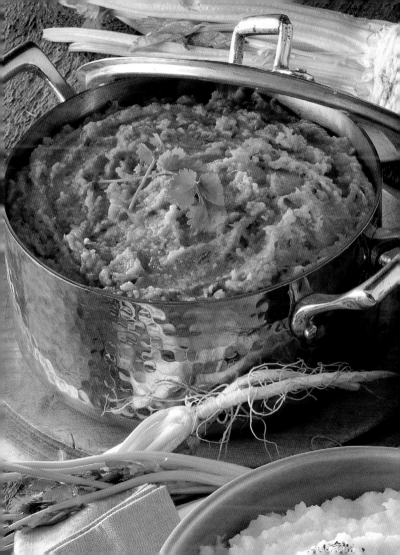

KITCHEREE

Preparation time:
15 minutes

Total cooking time:
30 minutes

Serves 6

INGREDIENTS

- 1½ cups (300 g/10½ oz) basmati rice
- 1½ cups (300 g/10½ oz) split mung beans (mung lentils)
- 2 tablespoons oil
- 1 onion, sliced
- 3 bay leaves
- 1 teaspoon cumin seeds
- 2 pieces cassia bark
- 1 tablespoon cardamom seeds
- 6 cloves
- ¼ teaspoon black peppercorns

1 Wash the rice and beans (lentils), then drain and set aside.

2 Heat the oil in a frying pan, add the onion, bay leaves and spices, and cook over low heat for 5 minutes, or until the onion is softened and the spices are fragrant. Add the rice and beans (lentils), and cook, stirring, for 2 minutes. Pour in 1.25 litres (1.3 US qt/1.1 UK qt) water, and season with salt. Bring to the boil, then reduce the heat to low and cook, covered, for 15 minutes. Stir gently to avoid breaking the grains and cook, uncovered, for 3 minutes, or until all the moisture has evaporated. Serve hot with Indian curries.

NOTE: To avoid serving with the whole spices left intact, tie the spices in a piece of muslin and add it to the pan along with the water. Discard when the dish is cooked.

SAFFRON RICE

Preparation time:
10 minutes + 30 minutes soaking

Total cooking time:
25 minutes

Serves 6

INGREDIENTS

- 2 cups (400 g/14 oz) basmati rice
- 25 g (¾ oz) butter
- 3 bay leaves
- ¼ teaspoon saffron threads
  (see NOTE)
- 2 cups (500 ml/17 fl oz) boiling
  vegetable stock (broth)

1 Wash the basmati rice thoroughly, cover with cold water and soak for 30 minutes. Drain.

2 Heat the butter gently in a frying pan until it melts. Add the bay leaves and washed rice, and cook, stirring, for 6 minutes, or until all the moisture has evaporated.

3 Meanwhile, soak the saffron in 2 tablespoons hot water for a few minutes. Add the saffron, and its soaking liquid, to the rice with the vegetable stock (broth), 1½ cups (375 ml/13 fl oz) boiling water and salt, to taste. Bring to the boil, then reduce the heat and cook, covered, for 12–15 minutes, or until all the water is absorbed and the rice is cooked. Serve with Indian curries.

NOTE: Saffron threads are the dried stigmas of the crocus flower. While available in powdered form, it is generally inferior.

CREAMY POLENTA WITH PARMESAN

Preparation time:
10 minutes

Total cooking time:
10 minutes

Serves 4

INGREDIENTS

- 1 teaspoon salt
- 2 cloves garlic, crushed
- 1 cup (150 g/5¼ oz) instant polenta (cornmeal)
- ½ cup (125 ml/4¼ fl oz) cream
- 40 g (1½ oz) butter, chopped
- ⅓ cup (35 g/1¼ oz) grated fresh Parmesan
- ¼ teaspoon paprika, and extra to garnish
- Parmesan shavings, to garnish

1 Bring 3½ cups (875 ml/30 fl oz) water to the boil in a large, heavy-based saucepan. Add the salt and crushed garlic. Stir in the polenta (cornmeal) with a wooden spoon, breaking up any lumps. Cook over medium heat for 4–5 minutes, or until smooth, stirring often.

2 Add half the cream and cook for 2–3 minutes, or until the polenta (cornmeal) is thick and comes away from the pan. Stir in the butter. Remove from the heat and stir in the Parmesan, paprika and remaining cream. Transfer to a warm serving bowl and sprinkle with paprika. Garnish with Parmesan shavings and serve at once.

NOTE: Polenta must be served hot to keep its creamy, light consistency.

INDEX